Inner Demons

Rahmaan H. Mwongozi

For information about special discounts available for bulk purchases, sales promotions, fund-raising, educational needs, public speaking, or use of this work or associated art/graphics in portion or entirety, please contact Empyreal Empire: press@rocsworld.com

Published in the United States by Empyreal Empire®

www.rocsworld.com

Names: Mwongozi, Rahmaan H., author
Title: Inner Demons: Blazing A Path To Happiness / by Rahmaan H. Mwongozi
Description: New York: Empyreal Empire, [2018]

HARDBACK ISBN: 978-1-7325618-0-9
PAPERBACK ISBN: 978-1-7325618-1-6
EBook ISBN: 978-1-7325618-2-3

Manufactured in the United States

Illustration: Havva (Eva) Karabudak
Cover Design: Amanda Morante
Formatting: Polgarus Studio

To my daughter, Yasmine Marie Mwongozi
You are the most extraordinary person I've ever met.
It is my greatest honor to be your father.

Contents

Years 6-8: Odis 1

Years 9-11: Anger & Defiance 11

Years 12-14: The Wonder Years 19

Years 14-15: The Human Perspective 27

Year 16: Part 1 - You Know Nothing… 31

Year 16: Part 2 - Friends? 35

Year 16: Part 3 - The Dog That Caught the Car 40

Year 16: Part 4 - What's Said in the Dark… 44

Year 17: Part 1 - Open Secrets 50

Year 17: Part 2 - Stay in Your Shoes 56

Year 18: Part 1 - The Dirty South 66

Year 19: Part 1 - You Can't Go Home Again 71

Year 19: Part 2 - Stay on the Path; Ask for Direction 78

Year 19: Part 3 - Pride Only Hurts 86

Year 22: Speak Up So They Can Hear You 93

Year 23: Houston, We Have A Problem 102

Year 23: Part 2 – Standing On My Own 113

Year 23: Part 3 – All Things Clearer in Time 119

Year 23: Part 4 – True Colors 131

Year 24: Part 1 – I Think It's Better That I Tell You Now..141

Year 24: Part 2 – A New Way to See Things 148

Year 24: Part 3 – All Good Things… 158

Year 24: Part 4 - Rock Bottom 164

Year 24: Part 5 - Left Behind... 167

Year 25: Part 1 - Adrift.. 171

Year 25: Part 2 – No Time to Be Afraid 176

Year 25: Part 3 – Complications... 183

Year 26: When Things Gets Real... 188

Year 27: Measure of a Man...200

Year 28: Part 1 – Make Yourself at Home 210

Year 28: Part 2 – Common Ground 217

Year 29: Too Many Straws 223

Year 30: That's The Bad Guy...242

Year 31: Part 1 – Hustle & Flow 246

Year 31: Part 2 – Chasing...252

Year 31: Part 3 - Recalibration..259

Year 32: Part 1 - Unexpected..264

Year 32: Part 2 – Closer to My Dreams 271

Where Ever You Go, There You Are 279

Author Bio 281

Acknowledgements

To my parents: Pamela, Rudi, & Rasheeda – Thank you for
your sacrifice, dedication, and love

To Ms. Bolling: Thank you for allowing me to play

To my friends: Thank you for your support, wisdom,
encouragement and patience

I would like to give special thanks to:

Stacey: Thank you for taking the most epic journey with me.
My only regret with this book is that it isn't long enough to
describe the full arch of our relationship. Our relationship has
grown into something I'm extremely proud of. My respect and
admiration for you has only grown with time. I'm blessed to
have you as a partner in parenthood.

Jennifer: Thank you for always being my dearest friend; more
than words can describe.

Dayna: Thank you for loving me and teaching me that I
deserved it.

Jenn: Thank you for the laughter you bring to my life and your
passion to embrace the best of everything.

Years 6-8: Odis

I sometimes wonder what would have become of me if I'd killed Odis O'Neal. Would it matter that I was just a child? Would the abuse I'd endured at his hands be enough to settle my debt to society? Or would I only be viewed as an angry boy who'd killed his stepfather? Perhaps the world would assume what I believed at that time — that my sins were the natural culmination of a young life that wasn't worth anything to begin with.

At the time, I blamed my parents for the abuse. If they had only done their job and stayed together, my mother wouldn't have married Odis. The memory of my father leaving stuck out in my mind, especially in the early days. I remember chasing him out of the apartment, his silhouette getting smaller and smaller as he put more distance between himself and us. It wasn't the last time I saw him, of course. He didn't walk out of my life completely—I suspect he came home that night—but I don't remember it. I just remember having two parents in the house and then having only one.

Until my mother married Odis.

Born in 1930s Arkansas, Odis was a product of his time. A stern and proud man, he lacked any sense of compassion, empathy, or humility. Any skill acquired by his hands came at the expense of his mind and vision. He wasn't a dumb man, but he was never free to find and express his full potential. He seemed to be aware of his limitations, but desperately wanted to be respected.

Whatever trust I had in my mother was muted by her introduction of Odis into my life. I loved my mother more than anything in the world, but at times I questioned her love for me. She always seemed so stressed and I suspected my presence was the primary factor for this. There were incredibly tender moments, like resting my head on her lap as she drove home from her second job of playing music at church. I remember closing my eyes and counting the turns and stops as we made our way home at night. However fond I was of those memories, they were never enough to alleviate the depression that consumed me after one of Odis's beatings.

With any gain made, he lorded over those he thought subordinate to him. Any challenge to his authority was met with meanness and cruelty; he didn't believe in sparing the rod. An elbow on the table would be met with a rap across the knuckles. Any accomplishment was greeted with jeer; as if any success achieved by my mother or me was more luck than dedication and hard work.

"What? So you think you're smart now?"

"That's what you get for hanging around me. Stick around long enough and you *might* be somebody someday."

"You weren't anything until I came along."

These were the sentiments of the man that was my stepfather. Life before Odis was much more bearable. I fondly remember trips to Portland to visit my mother's family. The savory crispness of fried chicken paired with an assortment of sweets sustained us while the passing countryside slowly revealed its hidden treasures. The 600-mile drive was an exodus away from the violence and desolation of my native Oakland; a brighter, cleaner world enticed me to forget all that I'd left behind.

The highlight of every trip was the building anticipation to see what I considered the jewel of northern California: Mt Shasta. I can't say exactly why, but I loved that mountain. Maybe because it seemed I could walk directly from the road to the top, or possibly due to the "magic" of having a snow-covered top in the middle of a hot plain. Whatever it was, the mountain and those trips were proof that there existed a bigger, more beautiful world beyond Oakland.

Perhaps it wasn't Oakland that I wanted to leave behind, but the pain and fear that it instilled in me. Maybe it was my desire to find a place where I was loved and wanted that made those rode trips so enticing. Like so many things lost in the haze of time, the answer has always eluded me, while other memories seemed to trouble every waking moment.

And yet/despite this, I had a very high opinion of myself. I don't think this was taught to me so much as it was reinforced. The name given to me at birth, Rahmaan Hussein Al-Soufi Abdullah Mwongozi, was more a title than a name. According to a hadith, which Muslims regard as records of the Prophet Muhammad, there are 99 names of God. Rahmaan: The Most Compassionate was even the first name on the list of names of Allah (God). When one of these names is chosen for a child, it is customary to add the preceding modifier "Abdul" — which means servant. I was not. Obviously, this was no mistake; I would be a servant to no one.

I used knowledge for my own, sometimes sinister, benefit and amusement. Once, I convinced a kid to take other children's shoes and toss them into a canal, knowing he would be beaten with a switch. I even pre-selected a supple, green vine especially for the occasion which I was more than happy to fetch so the appropriate punishment could be administered. Being compassionate wasn't something I aspired to, and at times my name was a source of embarrassment.

My primary pursuit in those days was trying to gather as much information as possible and use it to benefit me. I was unconcerned with what I was learning; it was the speed and volume of data that interested me. I developed a fascination with insect fights, all in pursuit of the question: why do things operate the way they do? All manner of creatures found their way into my jars, ants being my favorite. It was amazing to see such small creatures dominate larger foes by simply being unnoticed until they were ripping into their prey's flesh. Anonymity was a potent weapon.

This emerging psychopathy was neither bad nor good; it just was. Over the years, I realized there's just part of my psyche that always remains emotionally detached, concerned only with logic, causality, and effect. I need to know how and why things work so I can best understand how to make them work *in my favor*. But as much as I learned from watching insect fights, people were the greatest mystery.

*****

In Muslim school, there was a kid that everyone called Blacky. He was much darker than the rest of us and had a shiny face, likely due to the application of Vaseline by his parents. Aside from all of this, I remember that he was generally a nice kid—who didn't like being called Blacky.

The irony and hypocrisy of our immersion in overtly pro-black teachings while simultaneously bullying a kid because he was darker than us started to bother me. I simply couldn't make rational sense of it.

I vowed never to call him Blacky again. Despite the revelation that was revealed to me, I never spoke up when other kids were cruel. My only concern was with taking care of myself; everyone else had to find their own way. I understood my responsibility to be better, even if others were not. I still don't remember the kid's name.

All of these things were helping me to understand my place in the world. I'm not sure where my thoughts started, but I remember the questions it settled on: Why did God make me black? Why did he make us poor? Would my life be like this forever? This was the nature of my thoughts, even at such a young age.

This wasn't necessarily a question borne of racial insecurity, but simply to determine why I was in this world. I wanted to know why all the black people I knew didn't have much money and didn't live in the best neighborhoods.

It was this curious mind that Odis wanted to control. His chosen method for dealing with me was to beat me into submission whenever he felt I was getting too full of myself.

I remember one time coming home from school and the lure

of the corner store was too much to resist. The thought of a confectionary treat was the highlight of a long day of elementary school. Quickly settling on a Blow Pop, I had it unwrapped and in my mouth before I'd even had the chance to pay for it.

Money was always a touchy subject with Odis. According to him, all money in his house belonged to him and was subject to his control. He never forbade me from having my own money, but it was difficult for him to keep track of because I was secretive about how much I had at any given time. It never occurred to him that I could save gifted money for months. When asked how I was able to obtain certain things like candy, I would lie and say a friend gave me some at school. Having my own money was a source of power that I guarded fiercely.

Leaving the store with my change in hand and in sugar-aided bliss, I saw a flurry of movement just outside my peripheral view. Odis was driving by in his van, his eyes locking with mine. I knew that look. He continued down the road to collect my sister from daycare as I walked home in fear of what was to come.

When he came home, he beat me without saying a word. Each strike of the leather strap cut into me with rage and contempt. No matter where I tried to run, the strap was there. He beat me until I no longer had the will to run.

However bad the beatings, they were temporary. The worst part was the emotional abuse. He felt the need to constantly remind me that I would grow up to be nothing. Every action not to his liking was a sign I was doomed to prison.

As much of his wrath that I received, my mother would receive the same if not more. Not at the beginning though, that's not how abusers work, but over time. While never being physical

with her — he wouldn't have made it through the night alive—
he was quick to remind her that *he* was the best thing to happen
to her, and she was nothing before she met him.

She never had a thought or idea that he respected. The
criticism of her was constant. So were the accusations of
infidelity.

"Who are you putting makeup on for?!" he would often
accuse.

"I'm going to work, and I need to look professional."

In his mind, it had little to do with her desire to be more
successful and everything to do with some man she was
supposedly sleeping with. He never complained about the checks
she brought home, though.

Of course, not every day was bad. We had nice Christmases.
Thanksgiving was always a treat because we would go to his
brother-in-law's ranch, where I learned to shoot. It was nice
because the amenities were nice; almost like a consolation for the
misery that the rest of the year brought.

And he was very nice to my sister, Naima. Although she
wasn't his biological child, he adored her. She was only three, so
she couldn't get into that much trouble to begin with.

There was also the matter of my schooling. Odis grew up a
staunch Christian—he didn't support the Islamic school I was
attending. The fact that it took money out of the house was also a
key factor in his advocating for a change.

After consulting with his sister and brother-in-law, he made
arrangements for us to use their address in the affluent part of
town to enroll me in one of the better public elementary schools.
Years later my mother would try to convince me he really wanted

me to have a good education. It was something he would always pat himself on the back for.

This is how life was: some good, some bad, some awful. I hated him, and I hated my life. I began to view my mother in a different way. I couldn't understand why she would let this man treat me this way. I lost confidence in my mother during those years; it would take a long time for our relationship to be made right. I needed something to change. And that change would come one Friday evening.

My father arrived at our house to pick us up for our weekend together. Being kids, we had forgotten to pack our things and rushed to gather and pack for our time away. As my father walked into the house towards our room, Odis grabbed my father by the shoulder.

"Where do you think you're going?"

"I'm going to help my kids pack. Man, you better get your hands off me!"

"You just don't walk in MY house!"

At that moment, every boy's dream about his father came true. My father picked him up, slammed him onto the couch, and began to punch him—he was slaying my dragon!

I cheered as my mother yelled. As she reached for the phone to call the police, I pulled it out of the wall so she couldn't. I wasn't going to be robbed of this moment.

The man that had tormented me was no longer someone to be feared. He was only a small man that could do nothing more than lord over women and children. As soon as a man challenged him, my very own father no less, he crumbled under the pressure.

With haste, my father left and my sister and I were sent to

our room. It was unknown to me if I would have my weekend with my father, but what I had just witnessed would have been enough to make it ok. I didn't hear much coming from the living room, but I wasn't listening either. I was deep in my thoughts, knowing that something fundamental had changed.

My father soon returned with the police to collect his children and we had our normal weekend. For some reason it occurred to me that I never told my father the things that had come before. I don't know if I was scared or something else, but I felt dumb for not telling my father sooner. Of course, he would have saved me.

From that moment on, I was no longer afraid of Odis O'Neal. I was too tired of his act by this point. I was tired of the way he treated me and my family with his constant belittling and condescension. I'd always hated him and his beatings of me, but now there was something new: bitterness, anger and a lack of fear. It was a powerful concoction.

He was no longer the monster I assumed he was. He had been beaten by my father, the man whose blood flowed in my veins. I saw Odis as a weak man and a bully, something not worthy of respect or the life that he used to torment me and my family.

That was when I decided to kill him.

For weeks I thought about how to do it. This wouldn't be some reckless charge; I was going to take my time to ensure success. The idea of what would happen afterwards was of little concern; protecting myself in the present was my only concern. We didn't own a gun, so I needed another idea. Finally, I settled on a long kitchen knife. All I needed was the right trigger and opportunity. "Let him hit me again..." I thought. That was all I needed to set me off.

But that moment never came. With little fanfare, my mother soon announced that we were moving and she was getting a divorce. The shock of the news and the abruptness of it all left me confused and slightly uneasy. I could sense the anxiety in my mother and wanted nothing more than to comfort her and help in any way that I could. And although it was a sad and stressful situation, I gladly accepted the fate that lay ahead versus the one that would make me a murderer.

I think often about what might have been. I may not have actually gone through with killing Odis, but I hated him to the point that I wanted him dead. It was a blessing that we didn't have a firearm in the home, but even so, the effects of those years—good and bad—would stay with me for the rest of my life.

Years 9-11: Anger & Defiance

After Odis, I didn't trust my parents. I blamed them for allowing him to beat me. I blamed them for not protecting me and putting me in a position where I had to look out for myself. I saw them for what they were: poor people struggling to hang on in the world. The curtain had been pulled back on the wizard.

My child-like optimism was gone. I'd seen too many things and experienced far too much to maintain it. Drugs, crime, and violence were in ascendance. HIV was the new, mysterious disease making nightly news in the San Francisco Bay Area. These would be my killers if the Soviets and their nuclear bombs didn't beat them to it. I saw my world and hated it.

After 3 years in public school, I began to reject the entire enterprise. Upon entering public school after my years in a private institution, I was so advanced that my mother was given the option to place me in third grade, skipping second entirely. However, due to my late birthday and being younger than most children in my grade, she felt being that far behind in age would be a social hindrance. My achievement was sacrificed for the sake of social acceptance.

I felt suffocated by the lessons and curriculum. Learning new information was never the issue, but rather the environment and its rules. It seemed the entire enterprise was constructed to actually make me less intelligent. Everything was too slow, and the teachers were easily annoyed by questions that deviated from their lesson plans. My passion for learning ended at the entrance of the school door.

In fourth grade, I began to act out. I'd always possessed a strong personality, and though I had never won any outstanding behavior awards, I began to be willfully disruptive. Any sign of disrespect was met with an equal or greater amount of disrespect from me. Brushing aside my feelings prompted a more vocal expression of my perspective. At some point during that year, I received my first suspension from school.

By the time I completed fourth grade, I'd developed a reputation for being a difficult child. I imagine fifth grade would have been an extension of this trajectory if it weren't for Ms. Cheryl Bolling. From the very first day of class, she let us know she was in control; not in a threatening way, but as an extension of her confidence and trust in her methods and plan. She was nice, but you didn't want to know what was on the other side of that.

I felt as if she was placed in this world just for me. I sat at a table near her desk; there wasn't a child closer to her. At the time, I thought it was the greatest reward to sit so close to a woman I admired and respected. In hindsight, she probably heard of my reputation and wanted to keep a more watchful eye on me.

I couldn't imagine a better learning environment. Her philosophy was very simple: complete your work, stay out of trouble, and you were rewarded. Her rewards were autonomy to manage your work and pace, free time, and games. An entire section of class was dedicated to games, puzzles, toys, and even a computer.

We were tasked with generating a predetermined amount of work per week centered on our lessons: math, social studies, reading, etc. A culmination of weeks equaled a quarter. On the wall cabinet behind my desk was a chart that tallied our completed tasks per week towards our quarterly goal. As we each completed work within our lesson hour, any remaining time could be used in the play area.

This Montessori-styled setup was perfect for me: clearly articulated expectations and responsibilities with an unambiguous reward structure. What I appreciated most about this system was that it allowed me to do what I do best: analyze a problem, identify desired goals, and design a better way to achieve them. And to her credit, Ms. Bolling listened to me.

My sole goal in life was to master my lessons so I had free time to play. The quicker I completed my work and showed aptitude, the more time I had to myself. As I completed various lessons, I realized there was fixed and flexible time. Instruction-heavy lessons such as math and history had larger fixed-time components. Lessons, such as SRA Reading Laboratory lessons and book reports, were self-driven so free time was based on individual effort. There wasn't an hour within the day that I couldn't generate free time: greater aptitude generated greater rewards. The only thing better than a reward, however, is a greater reward, so I hacked the system.

SRA tiers were divided into 10 lessons, with each tier color coded for difficulty. Understanding that mastering lesson 10 was the ultimate goal of each tier, and each tier was to prepare one for the next tier, I began to skip all the lower lessons and tiers. As I saw it, there was no value in completing lower level lessons if I could master higher level ones. This allowed me to finish SRAs earlier in the hour, freeing up more playtime.

In a given week we had to read a book with at least 100 pages and write a one-page book report. Again, understanding that reading aptitude was the goal and knowing that a 200-page book was more complex and showed greater aptitude than a 100-page book, I offered to read a book with twice as many pages if I received double credit.

Ms. Bolling agreed, and on my next trip to the school library I created a reading list of every book that seemed interesting and contained at least 200 pages. Some of my peers would join me in reading longer books, realizing the value of this proposition. I soon began using free time earlier in the cycle to generate entire hours of free time later in the cycle.

Despite the relative calm provided by Ms. Bolling, the rest of my world was falling apart. Whether from the nightly news, the hushed and fearful tones of adults, or what I witnessed in the streets, I knew that I was living in the worst city imaginable. With an annual murder rate over 120 killings per year in my town of 300k, this wasn't my imagination. The danger was real, and the feelings of fear and anxiety were heavy.

Financial instability at home only added to my insecurities. While I greatly appreciate that my parents didn't hide their struggles, and have benefitted from understanding real life issues, it was, nonetheless, unsettling. I didn't have the words to articulate these feelings until I heard the music of a local rapper by the name of Too $hort.

One day on the bus ride home, a friend couldn't stop talking about this new rapper that he'd heard. As he handed me the white cassette tape labelled *Born to Mack*, he urged me to listen to it as soon as I got home. I don't remember what I expected when I put the tape in the player, but I will never forget the shock when the music hit my ears.

There was purity in the raunchy and vulgar themes and language. It was as if the soul of my city spoke to me through those speakers. Every thought, feeling, insecurity, or desire that I'd ever had was finally given life and air to breathe. To survive, I needed to adopt the bravado and unapologetic personality embodied by my new favorite emcee. I was given the blueprint for how to deal with my environment, and was committed to following it to the letter.

In hindsight, Ms. Bolling's fifth grade class was the calm before the storm. By the time I entered sixth grade, I had reached the end of my patience with being embarrassed and marginalized. I retaliated against every perceived slight, disrespect, or condescension.

My sixth-grade teacher seemed to have distaste for me, and the feeling was mutual. She was a smoker and constant coffee drinker, causing her breath to be particularly foul. When she refused to answer my questions, I refused to let the matter go until she addressed me. I didn't ask for permission to go to the bathroom—I just went and came back when I was done. I refused to follow instructions I didn't understand or that weren't clearly articulated. I was in control, not her.

This behavior would land me in the principal's office often. I liked Ms. Oyang personally, and we got along well on most days, but I'm sure she tired of seeing me in her office so often. In this way, I earned my second suspension from school, official cause stated as defiance of authority—something that would stick with me most of my life.

Classmates felt my anger. While I socialized well enough, I wasn't close to anyone on a personal level. Everyone understood I could be unpleasant when provoked, thus they tended to chill out when it came to confrontation with me. I never got into fights and wasn't a violent person, but I made sure to let people know not to push me. One day, however, I had to show that my bite was worse than my bark.

It was during a game of Four Square with some friends. There was a dispute with a kid about losing the match that quickly led to heated words. I refused to leave the space, so he pushed me. And to his surprise, I punched him in the face.

Separated by the other children before a victor could be determined, my bloodlust was unsatisfied. *He had to pay*, I told myself as I stormed away from the group. The sound of my own heart pounding drowned out all coherent thought as I re-entered the classroom searching for…something, anything I could use. I grabbed a baseball bat and a tantalizing feeling of satisfaction washed over me. *"I am the answer to your problem,"* it seemed to whisper to me.

Re-emerging onto the playground, I locked eyes with my prey. The fear I saw gave me a momentary feeling of satisfaction. But I wanted more. I ran towards him, bat in hand. Each zig and zag he made across the playground kept him just beyond my reach, but never far enough for me to give up my quest to make him pay for his disrespect. I chased him relentlessly until I eventually tired of it. I was suspended for the third time.

I needed help, but there was none from my parents. I don't think they understood what was going on with me, nor had a clue of how to relate to my issues. My father, having remarried, was focused on my new sister and providing for her and my step-mother. My mother had her hands full with two children, balancing her phone company job and earning extra money conducting music at church. Her idea of dealing with these issues was yelling and spankings.

They were doing the best they knew how to with the resources they had. Moreover, there was progress being made. I had a new sister who was adorable. My mother purchased our first house, although it was in an awful neighborhood. They were trying very hard to move the family ahead, and it was slowly but surely coming together. I understood that, but I resented their half-measures when it came to understanding and reassuring me. There was little time to constructively deal with my issues until there was no longer a way to avoid them.

There was no warning that my life would implode the evening my mother found a stack of unfinished homework assignments. The yelling and berating, while not unusual, were especially grating that night.

"Why haven't you done your work? You're going to end up pumping gas at a gas station if you keep going like this! You're going to complete every assignment that you didn't do!"

"But they're old. I can't turn them in. It's too late."

"I don't care. You'll do it anyway!"

I was angrier than I'd ever been. I'd been in school for three months and suddenly she wanted to take an interest in my schoolwork?

You're always the afterthought. She doesn't really care, just like she didn't care when her husband was beating you.

She was yelling so much that the words lost their meaning—only the volume registered to me. My instincts kicked in, believing I was on the verge of getting beat. *I have to get out of here*, I thought.

I ran for the front door but couldn't manage to unlock the deadbolt; the fear and anxiety paralyzing my ability to manipulate the mechanism. I was trapped.

Reversing course to escape through the back door, I practically ran into my mother. Her eyes flashed with anger as she descended upon me. I closed my eyes and reacted in the only way that felt natural – I punched my mother in the face.

Years 12-14: The Wonder Years

In the days before smartphones and mobile communication, an eleven-year-old could go missing for hours without parents having any means of contacting them. I loved the ability to disappear for an entire day.

My bike became my means of escape. It was easier to be alone than to deal with the complexities of relationships. I wasn't fond of other people and it seemed as if they felt the same. Unfortunately, long absences had consequences. I would often come home to the worried face of my mother.

"Where have you been?" she would ask. When I told her I was out riding my bike or playing video games, she would begin her interrogation.

"For hours? Who were you with?"

"Nobody. I went to play video games."

It never occurred to either of my parents that I didn't have close friends and that hanging out with people was counter to what I was trying to accomplish. In all honesty, I don't think they believed me and I didn't care. The only thing these discussions accomplished was making being away even more attractive.

I was creating my own path. I spent a good amount of time trying to filter the noise in my life. These were the years when I began to fully examine and reflect on everything I was learning. I found myself rejecting the infrastructure and boundaries placed around me; especially those imposed by religion.

I could neither accept a sorcerer God nor the costumed man telling me he was the deliverer of God's instructions for me. I dismissed the sectarian God and the God that required me to live on my knees.

Moreover, I refused to identify with victims. I couldn't help feeling repulsed by people allowing themselves to be abused and stepped on while begging for some unseen force to save them. Even worse were those giving up on this life and accepting meekness for fantasies of palaces and golden streets beyond the veil. I wanted nothing to do with those ideals.

Entering middle school during this period added another layer of variables to decipher. For the first time in my life, I was acutely aware of my blackness. What bothered me wasn't that I was usually the only black kid in many of my classes, but the fact that it was now a defining characteristic. I remember hurting my knee in class one morning and when the nurse arrived, asking which child needed help, my teacher casually said, "the black boy in the corner there…"

I never felt he intended it in any other way but to positively identify which child was in distress. However, as all eyes turned to me to acknowledge the obvious, I hated him. I hated him because he was a symbol of authority and to that authority, I was easily summed up — all uniqueness casually dismissed. I was just a black kid in a corner, hurting.

While there had been different reading and math groups in elementary school, everyone was still in the same classroom. By middle school, the implied sorting was made explicit. This systemic segregation was mirrored by the social bonds and choice of friendships that the children chose to make.

My exclusive status was also noticed by those not in my classes. I often heard remarks from other black kids wondering what classes I was in, because they never saw me during class time.

"You're in what class? Oh…you're real smart, huh?"

I felt pressure to choose between a world of academic excellence with children not interested in knowing me and a world where excellence was viewed as abnormal. Being a smart black kid was like being on the loneliest road in the world. My growing sense of isolation was acerbated by the fact that I didn't know how to actively make friends. I don't think I ever really cared for a friend personally until I met Remy.

He was the oddest kid I'd ever met. He was exceedingly "preppy," having attended one of the elite primary schools in Oakland. I don't recall him wearing much else besides a variety of brightly colored Polo shirts in those first few months. He was smart, confident, exceptionally friendly, and lacked any discernible sense of guile or pretense—all the things I felt I was missing.

Over the duration of seventh grade, Remy and I struck up a friendship. I was a bit wary at first, but he was an easy guy to like. We shared many of the same interests and talked about our families and different neighborhoods. His was the affluent nuclear family living in the good neighborhood, and mine was the broken family living in the hood. Slowly but surely, we became closer. Through him, I was able to meet a number of other kids. Some I liked and some I didn't. Because of Remy, I had finally found my social footing.

Despite these small outwardly gains, internally I was descending deeper into my own world. I hated school and everyone in it. I just wanted to be alone. By eighth grade, I began cutting class. I rarely cut a full day, but I would take periods off just to recharge the energy that was being drained away.

I took up stealing as a hobby because I was good at it. Not all the time, but when I wanted something—usually candy—I would go into a store and take it. Never one to be extremely reckless, I would study my mark before I ever made a move, success always assured.

It wasn't the prize I was after, though. The process of analyzing the system, devising a plan, and executing thrilled me. I was testing myself: sharpening my natural skills of observation, quick thinking, and problem solving. This was infinitely more valuable than whatever cultivated myths they were selling in school.

I began to reevaluate my previous conclusions about this country and the mythic figures elevated as demigods of civic science, virtue, and industriousness. I realized this country was built not only through hard work, but also by force and exploiting weaknesses in the system. The more prominent founders of this country were morally corrupt slave owners and rebels. One hundred years later, men who bucked convention and blazed new trails dominated the industrial revolution. Men and women who took stock of their circumstances and did something about it, whether it was fighting for power and control of resources or simply wanting equal standing within society, conquered the country's history.

Whether these men and women were good in the eyes of their peers was secondary to what they accomplished and the stories inspired by them. Many of my peers were consumed with guilt or anger regarding ancestors they'd never met and the circumstances under which they lived. While on a human level I could sympathize with the victims of historic crimes, I was never a slave or a holocaust victim. I was never lynched or denied my right to vote; I would never know the plight of women.

I was indifferent to it all. As far as I was concerned, the reason these people ever existed was to lay the foundation upon which I stood. I could only honor their lives and sacrifice by pushing forward and embracing all the opportunity they couldn't.

Of course, I never articulated these thoughts, but they made it difficult to adjust well to others. I felt as if I were always a step or three behind my peers in social settings. I was awkward, insecure and suspicious of them and their motives towards me. I was sure they could read my thoughts. Even though I had friends, I felt more alone than ever and sought deeper solitude to quiet the voices in my head.

My time began to be dominated by long bike rides, video games, and books. I loved my books. The written word was a magical vehicle that allowed me to enter new worlds, dimensions, and planes of existence. Countless nights found me studying our encyclopedia collection, consuming facts and building a knowledge base of the physical world.

Books of fantasy and magic allowed me to expand my mind and the realm of possibilities. I grew to understand that magic was the process of transforming thought into reality. I realized that knowledge and time were the missing ingredients to making visions manifest. Somewhere along the way, I began to question my own sanity.

As I journeyed further into the silence of my own mind, the one voice that I never tired of hearing was that of my step-mother. There was exoticness to her Philly sensibilities. In a world that I knew to be lying to me, she was blunt and to the point. She refused to let me slip into my own darkness; she challenged me to explain myself. Her intent was never to interrogate, only to enforce the habit of being purposeful in my thoughts and actions. Beyond teaching me to never follow the crowd, she also taught me to have a rationale for why.

She helped me understand that there were always layers and underlying motives. From her, I learned about consumerism and social programming and she made sure I knew how to guard my thoughts. If my father gave me passion, and my mother gave me dedication, my step-mother gave me perspective. Little did I realize, it would be the gift of perspective that would guide me out of the darkest place I'd ever know.

A ninth-grade school dance would be the scene of my breaking point. I'd spent the better part of seventh and eighth grades adding to a growing list of school suspensions and antisocial tendencies. Despite any social gains I seemed to make, I felt more isolated than ever. By ninth grade, I felt like a shell of a person. By that point in my life, I had a small group of close friends—Remy, Teo, Matt, and Jabari—but I only trusted them as far as I could see them. My paranoia and suspicion had become insurmountable. I was slowly losing my mind but I felt helpless, too afraid to ask anyone for help. I retreated so far into my own mind that I almost didn't return.

The night of the dance, I had a growing sense of unease beyond the usual adolescent nerves. Despite the large crowd, I felt more isolated and alone than I ever had. Every whispered word, spontaneous burst of laughter, or sideways glance had to be about me. Every joke had to be about how odd I was or how much I didn't fit in. I couldn't take it anymore.

I placed my head into one of the large subwoofers lining the stage, hoping to overpower the noise in my head. And in that instance, I finally understood one of life's many truisms: no matter where you go, there you are. I burst into tears.

My mother was concerned when she was called to pick me up from the dance early. I deflected her questions on the drive home in anticipation of retreating to my room and my thoughts. Once there, I climbed into bed, passing out from mental and emotional exhaustion. I didn't leave my room very often that weekend. I could barely find the strength to eat or do much else. I was depressed and couldn't bother to hide it anymore.

By Monday, I was a mess, too sick to go to school. As Monday transitioned into Tuesday and Wednesday, my thoughts were still consumed with thoughts of alienation and isolation. I couldn't help but wonder if anyone missed me or were happy to see me fall to the pressure. I was sure they were having a good laugh about it.

Why do you care? the voice in my head said. *If you're so sure they don't like you, why do you care what they think?*

That's a good point, I thought.

Stop feeling sorry for yourself and worrying about everything and everyone. Just do you. And if they don't like it, fuck them!

And that was that. Something shifted. I listened to that inner voice and prepared myself for school that Thursday morning.

It was the first of many conversations with my protective inner self. I actually thought of it as an entity separate from me, which probably meant I was truly crazy, but that's OK. I knew, when it came down to it, I was the only one I could truly count on anyways.

Years 14-15:
The Human Perspective

The wonderful thing about perspective is: to get a new one, you only have to let go of the old one. Hitting rock bottom is a strong motivating factor as well. I entered my high school years with a much different mindset than what I ended with in my middle school years. My mind was both open and closed to the world around me.

I wasn't quite sure who I was, but I knew who I wasn't. I was finally able to see my life wasn't that bad at all. More importantly, I began to understand my parents, if only a little better.

For years, I'd viewed my father as an example of how not to be a father. It wasn't that he and my mother weren't still together, but because his financial contributions were nonexistent. I knew intimately how hard my mother struggled to provide for us. Too many of her days ended with a prayer and plea for some path forward through the tough times.

I remember the late-night calls between my aunt and mother as she talked of crossing picket lines in order to do her job. She spoke of the pain her co-workers' taunts inflicted and their inability to understand that an industry strike check wasn't enough to feed her small kids. I could hear her crying through the walls when her heart was broken by someone she thought loved her.

I recall the notes of panic and desperation when she spoke about not having enough money to feed us through the end of the month. There were too many nights when she would wearily climb into bed, beaten down by the weight of her existence, only to wake the next morning to do battle in the corporate world for her children's well-being.

My father was a child of the 60s and 70s. He was a little black boy that grew up in blue-collar Oakland, California. He was the child of partiers and alcoholics. He was a child blessed with the gift of music. He was a man trying to do the best he could. I understood that my father's resources could only cover so much—for him that meant the basics for my half-sister and stepmother.

So it was of little consequence when my father told me he and the family were moving to Philadelphia. I didn't ask why. I didn't ask if I could go with them. I was indifferent because I knew it had nothing to do with me. I knew I wouldn't miss them and that was okay too; I'd see them again when I did. And I realized that without the fallback of being able to go to my father's house whenever my mother and I had an issue, I had to figure out a way to get along with my mother. Unsurprisingly, the answer was fairly simple: stop being an asshole.

I really didn't have fundamental issues with her. The best I could come up with was my disappointment that she couldn't come to any of my orchestra performances. But not only was she doing all the heavy work of providing for us, she was actually getting ahead.

Long gone were the days of welfare cheese and syrup sandwiches. We were no longer using generic ketchup mixed with water as spaghetti sauce. We'd grown from a family on the edge needing the good will of others to standing on our own. We no longer lived in apartments; we were property owners.

Our house may not have been in the best neighborhood, but it was ours. My mother did that. She didn't run home to the comfort of family and familiar surroundings when things broke down; she forged ahead through the storms. Like my mother, I turned my focus to the future and what I was going to make of it. In my newfound serenity, I was even able to get over Odis.

After their divorce, he'd owed my mother a decent sum of money. While short on cash, he was long on skill. They worked out an arrangement where he'd work off his debts. When she bought a house in need of repair, he was the man she turned to. In his mind, I think he thought he could possibly work himself back into her graces.

On any given day, Odis would be working on the house when I arrived home from school. Sometimes he would try to start up conversation, but my thoughts of taking a hammer to his face never made me very conversational. I hated him and I only needed to bide my time until I could exact my revenge.

So it was shocking when I saw him one day and felt nothing. He was had been working on some random chore when I arrived home from school and saw him. We exchanged the most basic greeting as I entered the house. Normally, the old feelings of hate and revenge would have consumed me, but on this day I dismissed his presence and disappeared into my room.

I had no feeling for him, positive or negative. He was just a thing that took up space and the space he occupied wasn't consequential. He wasn't worth the anger I'd stored up for him. I actually felt sorry for him.

Year 16: Part 1 -
You Know Nothing…

At sixteen, I learned there were two types of people in the world: people who liked me and people who didn't. I would do anything for those in the former; the latter could burn in a house fire. That mindset is what kept me going during junior year. I'd found a confidence that had previously alluded me and I was loving it.

Homecoming of 1992 didn't present itself as anything out of the ordinary, save for the venue of the local community college. It was always interesting to see peers dressed up, but there was nothing remarkable about this dance. The vibes were good, and I was having a decent time attempting my version of the latest dance moves. All was normal and conventional until I found myself dancing with a girl I'd never seen before. And at that moment, time stood still.

I'd never even seen her before—in fact, I'd never seen anyone like her. Her skin was the color of honeycomb. Her hair was dark brown and styled in a ponytail. Freckles dotted her face and high cheekbones. She was very pretty, but it was her eyes that captivated me. They were slanted and upturned with a distinctively Asian flair.

She seemed to look right into my soul—and was happy with what she saw. Even if I could have managed to speak, my mind was unable to form a coherent thought. But I didn't want to say anything; I just wanted to dance with her. At that moment, there was nothing else in the world.

We danced for who knows how many songs, until at some point, she vanished. She didn't say a word, she only turned and left. I was dumbfounded—not by her leaving, but why she had been there in the first place. As I stood on the dance floor, wondering what had happened, the sweet and fragrant smell of her hair clung like a haze to my thoughts.

When she finally returned from wherever she had gone, she grabbed my hand and took me back onto the dance floor. We danced until the end of the night. Neither of us said a word but still we spoke volumes to each other. Her eyes were pools of caramel that drew me in and threatened to never let me go. They told me that she could see me and that I was okay. In that moment, I trusted her completely and would do anything for her.

And then, just as suddenly as it began, it was over.

As the lights came on, she turned and walked away. Again, not a word was said. And that was it; she went her way and I went mine. It wasn't until I got home that I realized that I should have gotten her number. At the very least, I should have asked her name. It wasn't that I was scared to ask or doubted that she would have given these things, but it all seemed inconsequential at the time. As the weekend continued, I actually found it difficult to recall what she looked like. What didn't fade were the feelings of warmth and safety. For the first time in my life I felt whole, and I wanted that feeling again.

Monday morning started the same as every other Monday. I headed to first period English and took my seat in the front row. English was one of the few classes I wouldn't cut, because I enjoyed the class format. While the focus was standard literature, the teacher used open debate and discussions to examine the themes and ideas within a given piece of literature. I viewed the entire process as combat and my peers as fellow gladiators; I was determined to dominate.

When class was over, I packed my bag and a girl I'd never seen before started talking to me. As she talked, I realized that she'd been my classmate for nearly two months and I had no idea who she was.

She was cute, but I didn't know what to say. I barely heard a word she said, but she continued chatting away, oblivious to the fact that I had a war going on in my head. I wanted to be clever and charming, but I resigned myself to offering the appropriate responses at the right time.

"We have to get to next class, but you should call me tonight…" she said.

It was the last thing I expected her to say. Brilliantly, I used this to figure out her name.

"Sure…write your number down." And she did, name included.

I watched her walk away, wondering how I hadn't noticed her before. Dayna Gray—her name written neatly above her phone number—had talked as if we knew each other. How hadn't I noticed her before? She had a distinctive look—beautiful caramel skin with exotic almond-shaped eyes the color of honey. I wasn't sure why she was talking to me, but I would find out later that night.

Year 16: Part 2 - Friends?

After a day of dealing with the world, there was nothing that I wanted more than to talk to Dayna at the end of every evening. Very early on I knew she was the best friend I'd always longed for—I just never knew that's what I needed. But that was the beautiful part of our friendship—she knew what I needed even if I didn't.

We talked about any and everything. Nothing was off limits. We talked about our families, hopes, dreams, and fears. We talked about school work and our peers. We discussed the news of the day and the deeper philosophical questions that we had about ourselves and our lives.

Above all, we listened to each other. I found it incredible how easy life seemed to be when there was someone you could count on to tell you it would all be okay. She didn't say anything that I hadn't heard before. She wasn't a sage with otherworldly insight. She simply was the first person to hear my deepest insecurities and tell me that I wasn't crazy and that I mattered. She seemed to know me better than I knew myself.

Having one of our many late-night conversations, the subject of drinking came up. Up until this point in my life, I'd never been drunk. The most I'd ever had to drink was a sip of wine from my mother's glass once or twice. When I returned the question to her, she said that she was drunk when she met me.

"When was that?" I asked.

"The night of homecoming," she said.

"I met you at homecoming?"

"We danced all night."

"That was *you*?!"

"God, you're really dumb sometimes! You know that, right?"

The remainder of that conversation was filled with laughter, all from her, and admonishment of how dense I could be.

The realization of who she was made it easier to say yes when she called me Super Bowl. Her parents were hosting a party and she wanted me to attend. I hated the Cowboys, but I couldn't pass up an invitation to a Super Bowl party.

Unfortunately for me, I couldn't find a ride to her house and she lived pretty far from the bus stop. I thought about canceling, but I couldn't bring myself to do that. I was just going to have to suck it up and make the journey, limited Sunday bus schedule and all. It was warmer than I thought it would be, but I kept walking. The hills to her neighborhood were steeper than I'd hoped, but I kept walking. I wanted to turn back a number of times, but I kept walking.

When I finally arrived, tired and a bit sweaty, I was confronted with a scene I hadn't counted on: a house full of rowdy Filipinos. There were aunts, uncles, and countless others eating, drinking, and having a grand time. This was Dayna's maternal family, and I quickly understood that they liked to party. As I was introduced to everyone, forgetting names as soon as they were spoken, I felt nervous. I don't know what I expected, but I was uncomfortable.

I introduced myself to her parents, who were far friendlier than I was comfortable with, and found a place to sit.

Dayna chose a seat next to me and we settled in to watch the game. We talked about this and that, until we noticed that the game was getting out of hand. This was the epic game between the Cowboys and Bills—one of the largest routes in Super Bowl history. Everyone was marveling at the spectacle and really enjoying the party while waiting for the main course to be completed: spaghetti with crab claws.

There was a cheer when her mother finally presented the dish to the party. By this time, I was feeling hungry and decided to make myself a plate. As I stood, Dayna grab my arm and pulled me down.

"I'll make your plate," she said.

I saw other men making their own plates, but she was insistent about making mine. Maybe it was because I was a guest, but with the look she gave me, I knew not to argue. My lone protest was not to give me crab claws because I was allergic to them.

With plate in hand, I proceeded to eat and enjoy the game. It wasn't a good game, but it was highly entertaining and the food was delicious. I was having a pretty good time and whatever nervousness I may have had was gone—until it wasn't.

I started to feel very tired and my body hurt. It felt as if my blood was getting thicker. I was afraid I was going to throw up or pass out. Suddenly I was surround by worried faces, most prominently Dayna's.

Suddenly, Dayna and I both realized what it was. While I

hadn't eaten the crab, the spaghetti was tainted with its essence. I wanted to leave and go home, but she would not let me out of her sight. For the next hour, as I progressed through my allergic reaction, Dayna's face seemed to mirror what I was feeling. Eventually she relented and let me leave, apologizing continuously. She called me later to check on me.

"I didn't like you serving me a plate. I could have done that myself."

"I know you could have, but you were my guest and that's not what I'm about."

"It makes me uncomfortable to have that type of attention!"

"It's okay that you feel that way, but you're going to have to get over that. When you're with me, I'm going to bring you plates of food," she scolded.

I was getting angry, but I didn't know why. She was only trying to show me affection and consideration, but it felt unwarranted and undeserved. I was losing something, but I couldn't figure out what it was. Things were changing between us and it was unnerving.

We were able to laugh about everything, but there was no long conversation that night. I just wanted to rest. And the more I reflected on the events of that day, the more uncomfortable I became. I didn't like people waiting on me, and I was embarrassed by my illness. Moreover, the level of attention Dayna showed me didn't feel right. There was something very urgent about her that made me uneasy.

For the next few weeks, we continued as normal. Then one night, we were again talking about our love lives, people we had crushes on, and our lack of sexual experience. I'd only had sex for the first time about six months prior. Besides the fact that it was a fluke occurrence, it was highly unremarkable. I barely remembered her name.

"We should have someone we can explore with and learn what we're doing," I said jokingly.

"That's a great idea," she said.

"Now all we need to do is find people that's cool with that!" I laughed.

"Well….we could always practice with each other."

As the implications of what she said lingered in the air, my mind was filled with bewilderment, excitement, and nervousness. I'd casually thought about what it would be like to be in a relationship with her, but I'd never thought about having sex with her. Our relationship had long passed the point where anything physical held any relevance over the importance of what we were to each other.

"You think that way about me?"

"You're alright!" she laughed. "So, what do you think?"

"What do you think I think?"

Silence was followed by silence. And more silence—the gravity of the moment seemed to weigh on us.

"So…"

"So…when do you want to get together?" I asked.

"Soon…"

"How about we cut class tomorrow and hang out at my house?"

"Sounds good."

"Cool….want to meet at 35th and MacArthur at 8:15?"

"OK."

Year 16: Part 3 - The Dog That Caught the Car

It seemed strange to see her on this particular corner. I'd spent nearly every day of the past ten years crossing this intersection coming and going to various schools, but this was the first time I'd ever seen her here. It was not unlike randomly running into a celebrity at the grocery store, an exceedingly normal situation made extraordinary by their mere presence.

As we rode the bus back to my house, few words were shared but none seemed appropriate. I was unusually aware of her presence. As I watched the rain stream down the window, I could feel her leaning into me, resting her head against my shoulder. She smelled like my favorite dream.

It was a cold, rainy day, so as soon as we arrived at my house, I built a fire. As the fire grew, we talked about inconsequential things and random nothings. I cooked her a breakfast of scrambled eggs and toast, exceedingly proud of the perfect eggs I was able to produce. We were two young people avoiding the reason they'd decided to get together in the first place.

Eventually, I walked over and kissed her. Even now, nearly

twenty-five years later, this moment still gives me butterflies. As I looked into her amber colored eyes, I understood that this moment was the one I'd coveted since I'd laid eyes on her all those months ago. The girl of my dreams kissing me in my living room. I grabbed her hand and led her to my room.

I knew my life would never be the same. I started to miss her before she even left my house. I was consumed with a hunger and yearning that I'd never experienced before. I couldn't help but notice the smell of her hair as she passed through each room, as if to leave me a parting gift. I held her firmly as she kissed me. I wanted to say something, but I couldn't find the right words to express how I truly felt.

I wished I'd said something. Holding on to those unspoken thoughts burned an acidic hole in my mind that was painful to bear. We had made a pact that this act would not change our friendship. We were only intending to have a little fun, then turn our attentions towards our respective crushes. This would be our little secret.

For the remainder of the evening, these thoughts burrowed through every other thought that attempted to form until there was nothing left. They suffocated me as they made their way into the pit of my stomach. I was consumed with thoughts of her; my only solace was the smell of her on my pillow.

I arrived at school the next day with a sense of opportunity. Somewhere in this day, the right time would present itself to share a special moment with the girl I'd shared the most wonderful moment of my life with.

As I eagerly approached my class, I saw them. Dayna was standing arm in arm with her crush. She smiled at me as she walked into class, but when she saw my face, the smile was replaced with a look of confusion and maybe a touch of guilt.

I was in a foul mood. I was losing control and that was no longer an acceptable option for me. What was I so upset about anyway? She was perfectly within her rights to pursue any relationship that she chose, but I wanted her for myself.

Consumed with my own thoughts, I was largely oblivious to the conversation around me. As the class discussion was proceeding without my usual input, someone felt compelled to seek my opinion thus lighting the fuse to a simmer powder keg.

I gave my opinion, was presented with a rebuttal, and offered my counter. As this back and forth continued, my usual "restraint" was rapidly being depleted. And then I heard it...

"Oh shut up!.....hahahaha!"

As I turned to look at Dayna, the sense of betrayal and hurt boiled over. I no longer saw my best friend, I only saw an enemy that needed to be destroyed.

"Who do you think you're talking to?!"

The cold fury was on display for all to see. An eerie silence descended upon the room as everyone seemed to sense that there were deeper issues at play and they wanted no part of it. She just looked at me, knowing something had changed. And then it was over; I shut down and the discussion moved on without any further participation from me.

For the rest of the morning, I alternated between feelings of sullenness and rage. I could forgive her desire to date someone else, but she tried to embarrass me, and that was a cardinal sin. As far as I was concerned, she was dead to me. As lunchtime approached, I slowly regained a semblance of composure, but the feelings of betrayal lingered.

At lunch, when my boys asked where I was the day before, I didn't hesitate to discuss in vivid detail what had transpired. I'm not sure what can be expected of kids when it comes to their sexual adventures, but even at the time, I was aware of the contempt and malice with which I spoke. But I felt better—that was my only concern.

Year 16: Part 4 - What's Said in the Dark...

We avoided each other for the next few days. We missed our nightly calls and did our best to give each other space around school. It was starting to become unbearable for me. It all seemed silly and petty. I missed my friend.

I won't take credit for initiating dialogue, because knowing myself, I was probably too proud to do the obvious. Somehow or another, we resolved to talk everything out.

"What's your problem with me?" she asked.

"I really don't want to talk about it. It's something I need to handle on my own."

"It's because of him," she said casually. "I could tell you were bothered by it."

"It's my own problem."

'It's not your problem, it's *our* problem. You always do that: when you're bothered by something you just shut down."

"Hey...I knew what it was. I just need to get myself together."

"Why are you pushing me away? You're my best friend," she

44

implored. "We're supposed to be better than this."

"I just wish you weren't with him in front of class. You can see who you want, but I don't really want to see it."

"Then just say that!" she raged. "Stop acting as if you don't care all the time. I know you better than that. Give me some damned credit."

What began as a tense conversation full of hurt quickly moved into something that we hadn't experienced in a long time: awkwardness. For all we were saying to each other, we couldn't bring ourselves to say the things we really wanted to say and hear.

Now was the time to tell her that I'd told my friends about our hookup. I could visualize the decision to tell her or not to tell her as if they were two separate paths and I stood at the fork. I could tell her and risk undoing all the work we had just done, or I could hope it never came out. So I did what any sixteen-year-old boy would do—I kept quiet and hoped it would never come out.

As the weather warmed, so did our relationship. Any lingering uneasiness quickly dissipated. All was well in the world as the school year approached its conclusion. Feeling the spirit of the season, I began lending my contributions to an end-of-the-year school event.

Enjoying the comradery of my classmates, seeing Dayna enter the auditorium and approach the stage filled me with warmth. I jumped off the stage to greet her, but the look on her face told me something was off.

As the tears, betrayal, hurt, and anger rose in her eyes, I felt a sense of panic. She'd found out I'd gossiped about our time together. As she pleaded with me to understand why I'd done it, my mind was swirling. I was sorrier than she could have imagined at the time, and I grasped for a way forward.

Never one to show weakness, I replaced emotion and compassion with cold indifference.

"Hey, it is what it is."

She stared at me.

I stared at her.

As the emotion drained from her face, I saw our friendship evaporate. Fire and fury grew in her eyes and a cold void enveloped my heart.

Stick to the code, I warned myself.

All contact between Dayna and I ceased. Word spread of what I'd done and sides were chosen. In the eyes of most of the girls that knew, I only confirmed and solidified my hard-earned reputation of being the worst guy.

I was done. I was neither heartbroken about it nor angry. I understood why she was upset, and knew she was justified to feel that way. I didn't care. I was aware of the damage I'd done but there wasn't anything I could do about it. An apology seemed too small to do any good. Why bother?

Summer couldn't come fast enough. The tension in English class would ebb and flow depending on the day. I just wanted to be away from her. Seeing her every day was a constant reminder of the worst elements of my being, and I didn't need that.

Dayna was widely considered one of the most artistically gifted students in our class. She wrote calligraphy by hand and even had a small business creating custom scrapbooks for friends and family. When she asked to have my book for a few days I was excited about what she would create, but mostly glad that an opportunity to apologize had materialized.

Not nearly as talented, I quickly wrote my apology and returned her book in anticipation of seeing what she had to say. Each morning I would ask for my book and she would calmly say that it wasn't ready. She would smile and encourage me to be patient. As the days accumulated, my anticipation to see what she was working on was quickly reaching a fever pitch. Even more maddening was that she would lend my book to other people to sign for me but made sure I never had an opportunity to take a peak.

And when I thought I couldn't take it anymore, she approached me one afternoon and handed me the book. As she returned it to me, she gave me explicit instructions to not read it until I got home. As she turned to walk away, I caught the scent of her hair and was helpless to do other than what she'd instructed.

I'm not sure which was racing faster, my car through the streets or my heart in my chest. I missed my friend immensely and wanted nothing more than to put this chapter behind us. The thought of the wonderful things she must have created, fueled my imagination as to what our relationship could be going forward. As I thumbed through the book, my heart stopped as I found the page.

YOU ARE THE DEVIL!!!

Whatever illusions I had of us mending our broken relationship evaporated. Instead of a long and loving letter about our friendship and moving forward, I was instead given an account of how terrible I was as a human being. She spared no expense: she paid every slight and mistreatment of her back to me with interest. Her writing consumed two full pages of my book.

As I continued to read about my lack of morals, my cold heart and my calloused indifference to someone that "took a chance on me", a sensation that I hadn't felt in years began to creep up my spine. The warmth spread up my neck and over my head, until it covered my face in what I could only describe as burning rage.

I was stunned. I just didn't see this coming. She knew that I was sorry, right? She had to have seen my apology days before she could have completed all of it. How could she not see how I truly felt? Each additional question served as fuel for the inferno that raged within. If this is how she wanted it, to be my enemy, then all-out war was what it was going to be.

Enraged, I walked to the kitchen with a plan. If she was going to embarrass me, then I had something for her. Opening the spice cabinet, I collected the ingredients of my revenge: Worcestershire sauce and oil. From the refrigerator I collected mustard, vinegar, ketchup and mayonnaise. Fragrant shower oils and dirt from the backyard were added to the brew I was concocting. And when it was complete, I knew this vile mixture dumped over her head would be the perfect way to express how I felt about her.

Never one to miss an opportunity to cut school, I made a special point to be present on the last day. I had revenge to collect. I would ambush her as she walked to her afternoon class. It was a semi secluded area on campus with plenty of bushes to conceal me as I lay in wait.

When the time arrived, I took up position. The mixture, having ripened overnight, was especially noxious. I thought of nothing as I waited, oblivious to any and everything except my pride and ego. She was going to learn that I wasn't the one to take shots against.

And then I saw her. She was walking alone, books in hand with a self-satisfied smile on her face. This was it; the time had come...

I didn't move.

I stared at that smile and I remembered how she smelled. I remembered how her lips tasted and how she would laugh with me and tell me wonderful things late at night.

I couldn't move.

I knew that everything she'd said about me was true. I was the worst person. I was proving it at that very moment. This whole situation was my fault because I was too afraid to tell her I loved her.

I watched her as she made her way into the building and out of sight, oblivious to the conflict that was transpiring in the shadows. I sat there an extra moment, consumed by my thoughts and feelings. As I made my way out and on to my next class, I tossed the bottle of liquid into the nearest trash can.

I'd hurt her before, but that was all by accident. This was something much different and darker. This was a place I was afraid to go. This was a place that I wouldn't go; because I loved her.

Year 17: Part 1 - Open Secrets

Even though I considered myself a loner, I found that I really enjoyed being around people. Their energy inspired and motivated me. In turn, I used my energy and gifts to protect them when and where I could. This proved to be an important trait the summer before my senior year.

Most of my boys had started dabbling in alcohol and marijuana. These weren't cries for help, signs of trouble, or any other type of cautionary tales, just young people having fun and experimenting. Nearly everyone had high GPAs and plans for higher education. I was completely sober, so my role was to be look out for everyone else.

I was happy to be the designated driver for all of our evenings out. And seeing that my boys' parents had really nice cars, this was a win/win for everyone. I also took it upon myself to play devil's advocate when we were coming up with our schemes. It was always better to think through various scenarios and our responses to them, rather than being caught off-guard if something went down. We were brothers, and we looked out for each other.

In that moment, life was good. Just one more year and I was free to pursue my own course in the world, leaving the pain and frustrations of Oakland behind me. Given all that we'd been through, my mother was cautiously optimistic for what lay ahead for me. I'm sure there were times when she doubted I would reach this precipice; at times I'd wondered the same, but here we were. As the summer progressed, I thought about Dayna from time to time. She lived in the same neighborhood as Jabari, and I drove near her home often.

Sometimes I had an urge to toss a rock through the large window in her living room, but I would let that feeling come and go. Why prove myself to be a bigger asshole than I already was? There was also no need to do anything to tie myself to this town longer than I had to. There was nothing worth more than the future that I wanted for myself.

Senior year would be my victory lap for a life well navigated. There was a college waiting for me somewhere, most likely down south, and I couldn't wait to be there. I needed no extra complications that would require me to stay. My only thought when I arrived for school the first day of senior year was to run out the clock and get out of town with a win.

This was the first day of the rest of my life. I'd ascended to the pinnacle of childhood. Each period offered its own version of a new beginning. But as I hurried to the sixth and final period hoping to not be too late, I found myself staring into Dayna's eyes.

The look on her face mirrored my feelings: this was NOT how I wanted to end my day and I really don't want to do this here and now. We looked at each other, weighing the situation. Was there to be a scene? Was there lingering anger?

"Just grab the two remaining seats right there," said our economics teacher, Mr. Gade.

The two remaining seats were side by side.

"There's nothing else?" we said simultaneously.

"Is there a problem?" inquired Mr. Gade.

We quietly took our seats, resigned to our collective fate. This was going to be the longest year of my life. I just needed to keep my mouth shut and get out in one piece. So when the final bell rang, I hurriedly packed my things in a bid to escape this horror.

At the front of the quad, I waited for my friends to gather. There were a few that I'd promised a ride home to, including the sister of a friend who I thought was very cute. As we waited for the full group to form, Dayna suddenly sprung into our midst as if the passing breeze had deposited her there silently.

"Can I talk to you?" It was more of a statement than a real question.

"OK..." I followed her and braced myself for what I knew to be an awkward and possibly incendiary confrontation.

"We need to put all of this behind us and bury the hatchet."

I hesitated; this was not expected.

"I'm sure you want to bury the hatchet in my head," I laughed nervously.

"Maybe," she laughed. "But we can't go through this whole year hating each other."

"I'm really sorry about everything that happened!"

She just smiled at me.

"It's OK. Can you drop me off at home?"

"Sure."

And with that, it was over. All the hurt feelings seemed to be forgiven. But I didn't trust her; sure this was some type of trap. However, I finally had the opportunity to speak my mind and ask for my forgiveness. If she was willing to accept my apologies, I had to be willing to accept that she was okay with me.

As we rejoined the full complement that was now waiting for us, more than one suspicious glance was cast her way. She walked in silence and seemed to pay none of it any mind. Upon reaching my Chrysler Caravan, everyone piled in with Dayna calmly walking to the passenger door, opening it, and settling in as if she were a conquering queen.

With everyone buckled in, I began to call out the logistics of the drop-offs.

"You're dropping me off last," Dayna said.

I would be lying if I said that I wasn't getting slightly annoyed by her entitled behavior. We had just become cool again, now fifteen minutes later, she's acting like the queen bee in my hive.

I drove everyone home wondering the whole time what Dayna's game was. As I pulled away from her house, the smell of her hair filled my senses from when we hugged goodbye.

I had no idea what the next days and weeks would be for me. That brief moment of reconciliation only seemed to usher in a period of constant torment. I began to dread sixth period. Government & Economics was a class that necessitated discussion, which was the free pass Dayna needed to take shots at me at will.

There was nothing I could say that wouldn't elicit some type of response from her, ranging from a total rejection of my point or a critique about my phrasing of a point she agreed with. The class was comprised of about twenty girls and only two boys including myself, and at times, it felt as if she had a built-in chorus of supporters spurring her on. I knew I was in a losing battle.

All of this was in spite of the fact that we were, more or less, on normal speaking terms. We weren't at the level we once were, but enough to where we could hold conversations with each other and not be weird about it. It was mostly confined to the classroom, but there were occasional evening conversations— though not with the frequency of before.

And then something changed. The barbs that she would throw my way didn't sting anymore. The teasing and playfully dismissive attitude during discussion was no longer able to get under my skin. I was simply beyond it, consumed with one singular thought:

This is the girl I want to spend the rest of my life with.

This was not to say that I abandoned my positions or toned down my passions for what I said. I simply no longer acknowledged the sly jokes at my expense. I'd pause, making sure she had all the time she needed to say what she needed to say with a moment or two to let her comments echo in the silence. I would let the awkwardness of the moment linger and then continue with my point. When we spoke directly, I would just ignore them.

I had my friend back; my best friend. I was in love with her, but I was no longer weighed down and confused by it. I wasn't afraid of saying it, I just realized that it wasn't as important as actually loving her. Being a true friend to her was the mandate; caring for her regardless of how the relationship grew or changed. While I was happy to be in this place, I was far from content.

On the last day of school before winter break, Dayna and I spent the majority of the period talking to various friends that we wouldn't see for the next two weeks. These conversations progressed organically, and Dayna and I were inevitably part of the same ones. Eventually we found ourselves quietly talking to each other alone.

I stared into her eyes, reminded of how easily I could be rendered speechless by their gaze. It always felt as if she was looking into my soul; reading my deepest thoughts. There was a time when I would have been scared, but not now. I'd found the way forward that had alluded me for so long.

"I'm going to miss you."

She sat at her desk quietly, looking down at her hands folded on the table in front of her.

"Why?" she asked, still looking at her hands.

"Because I love you."

She looked up at me.

The look on her face wasn't shock. It wasn't even happiness. What I saw was a sense of calm mixed with pride and relief.

"I love you too."

Year 17: Part 2 - Stay in Your Shoes

As Dayna and I settled into our new dynamic, I felt a sense of ease. I had the girl of my dreams, a renewed sense of confidence, and my pending graduation from high school. While I never doubted my ability to reach these goals, they signified my mastery of my waning time in Oakland and my childhood. It was time for me to turn my attentions towards the chapters to come: college and moving away from home.

For someone so intent on going to college, my habit of cutting school was a bit ironic. But one bright March morning found me at home with Matt. There was a slight commotion at the front door, and I opened it to see the day's mail had been delivered—including a large envelope embossed with the Morehouse College seal.

A lifetime of work and struggle was contained within the contents of this package. *There's a bit of weight here*, I mused. That was a good sign. As Matt watched in eager anticipation, I scanned the first few lines of the enclosed letter: I was accepted into the fall class of 1994.

The nervous energy I was struggling to contain evaporated in that instant. As I hugged my friend in joyous abandon, I couldn't help but imagine what lay ahead. Morehouse and Atlanta would be the road to a new, brighter future. And the best part was, Remy and Jabari would be joining me there. We just had to get through the rest of high school. Dialing my mother's office number, I knew what this news would mean to her.

For seventeen years, her thoughts of me were filled with worry, fear, love, sacrifice, and optimism. To have the opportunity to repay her sacrifices and allay her fears was a gift that I'd always hoped for. To hear her elation while receiving this good news meant more to me than anything else.

With high school graduation approaching, I began to feel a sense of accomplishment and relief. I never doubted that I would graduate, but I was glad that it was finally on the horizon. I was also glad to be able to push back on the narrative that young black men struggle to graduate high school.

Adults don't understand that their anxieties about black boys graduating high school—or living to see eighteen—can sometimes do more harm than good. It's an extremely pessimistic environment which makes it difficult to maintain motivation and contributes to a sense of hopelessness.

With this chapter behind me, I decided that now was the time to have my first drink. Until now, I'd avoided alcohol because I didn't want to interfere with the work I had to do. I didn't feel that I'd earned the right to relax at that level. While some of my friends were drinkers and high achievers, I didn't feel it was right for me. This would be a treat for myself.

When we were invited to a party in Black Hawk, Ca., I knew how I was going to celebrate. I quickly polished off my bottle of Cisco on the way to meet with another group. Someone offered me a bottle of cran-apple juice and vodka that I enthusiastically became acquainted with. Once at the party, I may have had a beer or something else, but the only thing I wanted was to get to the pool house where the DJ was spinning.

I was having the time of my life. I was on another world. The only things I could feel were amazingness and the music. That is, until I started to feel the room spinning a little too fast. Suddenly, this party wasn't the great time I thought it was. The only thing I wanted to do was find a soft place to lay down; just for a bit.

I left the pool house trying to reach the main house, making sure I didn't fall into the pool. Once in the house, I saw a couch in the game room that looked perfect for passing out. *A calm place to relax for a while; about fifteen minutes*, I told myself. When I awoke, I was sure of two things: I had been asleep for much longer than fifteen minutes, and I was about to be sick. I was going to be very sick.

I must have looked like a mess, because everyone I passed on the way to the patio stopped to ask me if I was alright.

"I'm fine…" I assured them. "I just need some air."

Once outside, I surveyed the scene. The pool and patio were no place for me in my current state. I also couldn't remember where the bathroom was. I did, however, think that the bushes near the main house were calling my name. I gingerly made my way behind them and let go of everything my stomach was fighting hard to get rid of. Every retch simultaneously made my stomach feel better but made my head feel worse. I became "that guy" at the party.

The feeling of floating was now a feeling of drowning. I just wanted to get home. It didn't take long to round everyone up. Word had spread through the party about my condition and Remy had already started the process of getting us out of there. As always, the crew was there to take care of a fallen man. As Remy pulled away from the house, he only had one request of me: let him know if I needed him to pull over.

The day of prom, Matt and I drove our cars to San Francisco so they would be available after the party. That evening, we collected our dates and the rest of our party in a limo for a pre-prom dinner in Sausalito.

This was our first experience with haute cuisine. And it was terrible. It was a classic, minimalist presentation with exceptionally petite serving sizes. While we didn't enjoy dinner, we were enjoying the company and the event. The evening ride across the Golden Gate Bridge back into the city only served to highlight the ambiance of the evening. Dayna was the most beautiful I'd ever seen her.

The party at the Grand Hyatt was amazing. Throughout our high school years, our class was able to accumulate a sizable war chest and it showed. It seemed as if no expense was spared. We greeted friends, took pictures, laughed, and danced the night away. The final dance of the night with my beloved was perfect beyond words. This was living.

As the party closed down, Matt and I gathered our dates to head home. We had an early day the next morning with plans to go to the local amusement park. I'm not sure how it started but as we drove across the bridge back to Oakland, we began to drive more aggressively. Before long, we were in a flat-out race. At three in the morning, traffic was light. I was having a grand time, while Dayna was increasingly worried at what was happening.

About two miles from our exit, Matt passed me, and I had no hope of catching him. As I exited the freeway, I saw him waiting at the off-ramp light and I saw my chance. If I take the lead now, he would have no opportunity to regain the lead until we reached his house. As I ran the red light, I realized my mistake too late.

BAM!!!!!

I had managed to find the one other car on the road, and put my Dodge Caravan in its path.

The car was inches from me after slamming into the driver's side door. Everyone was in shock. When the car backed up from the point of impact, I panicked and floored it. I was out of there with thoughts of losing the other car in the streets of Oakland. I drove another two blocks, made a left turn and stopped; my reasoning was back online, and I knew it was wrong to run. I had to face what I'd done.

Discussions with the driver, a call to my mother, and an immense sense of guilt ended my prom night. I won't say I didn't know why I did it because I did: I hated to lose. If there was an opportunity to win, I was taking it.

But what was that worth? I thought.

I could have killed someone; the least being myself. How would I have felt if I'd hurt someone or, worse yet, the girl I'd worked so hard to be with? The thought shook me to my core. Luckily for me, no one was hurt, and we were able to work out a deal with the driver regarding expenses. Despite the danger I had put everyone in, both my mother and Dayna showed me nothing but compassion and understanding.

I was lucky to make it to graduation day. The wild and crazy events of the previous weeks served as a reminder to not lose focus; events could easily spiral out of control if I didn't remain vigilant. My graduation was a classically beautiful June day in Northern California: warm with a cool breeze.

This signified the end of my youth—even more than my upcoming eighteenth birthday. A lifetime of effort, fear, hope, and perseverance had brought me to this point, and I was happy to see it come and to leave it in my rearview mirror. There were greater adventures over the horizon, and I was eager to get to them.

This was a joyous day for friends and family, and I was happy to be carrying our family legacy forward. I was happy to see the look of pride in my parents' eyes. Noticeably absent were my father's parents, although they lived less than ten miles away. They were invited, but they declined.

My grandmother informed my mother that she would be attending the graduation of my deceased aunt's, best friend's, daughter's graduation that was being held that same day (my father's sister died of cancer about five years prior).

One would think that seeing their first grandchild graduate high school would mean something special to them, but I guess seeing their dead daughter's friend's daughter graduate was more dear to their heart. I didn't feel a way about it, but I did take note.

I didn't get to see my grandparents that day, but I did get to see Tom Hanks give our graduation address. I was a huge Tom Hanks fan. I remember watching *Bosom Buddies* in the evenings on Channel 2. The year prior to my graduation was the year that he did *Philadelphia* and I thought it was the most amazing film

I'd ever seen. He and Denzel Washington put on a performance for the ages.

He'd graduated from my school in 1974 and somehow our class was lucky enough to have him at our graduation in commemoration of his twenty-year anniversary. Now, I was seated a few yards away from someone I admired, and it felt like he was speaking directly to me about the life that lay ahead. This was very special to me because again, I was a huge Tom Hanks fan.

My dream to leave Oakland was just a few months away. It was sad to be spending the last few weeks with many of my friends, except for Remy and Jabari who were attending Morehouse with me. Plus, many of the people we hung out with on a regular basis were also attending school in Atlanta. When added to the friends that were a year or two older than us who had already made the journey to Atlanta, our social network was largely intact.

The one thing that I would miss, however, was Dayna.

She was attending San Francisco City College where her mother worked and tuition was free. Her plan was to complete her associate's degree before transferring to a university. As the number of days we had left dwindled, I became increasingly worried about us.

I was conflicted. On one hand, this was the girl I wanted to marry. For the past two years, this was the vision that I had for us. On the other hand, I was moving to the other side of the country for college. I knew I would want to date and give in to my inner desires. The beauty of the women in Atlanta was discussed in near mythical terms. Why wouldn't I want to take part in that?

We spent the hours, days and weeks of the summer just being with each other. We knew that things would change, but we didn't want to think or talk about it too much. It was too hard to bear. Now was the time to *be*.

One night we decided to go to one of the lookout cliffs to see the city lights. It was getting late, but we wanted to be away from other people. Our time together was running out. We didn't plan to stay long because her curfew was coming due, but my car got stuck on a berm on the trail. As the time rolled by, I started to panic knowing that I had Mr. Gray's daughter out well past curfew. There would be hell to pay.

How was I going to explain to him why I had his daughter out hours past curfew? I wasn't afraid for my safety, but you can never be so sure when you're dealing with a man's daughter.

After a tow truck that happened to pass by helped get my car unstuck, we drove to her house. I parked the car, walked to the front door with her, and it opened to reveal an angry Mr. Gray. We walked in quietly and knowing we were going to get it.

I took all the blame. I explained how we were on our way home, but I had driven the car into a ditch and had to wait for a tow. I was a little fuzzy about where this ditch was and how I got in it. I didn't see much value in mentioning those details; we were in enough trouble.

He thanked me for the explanation, despite his anger, but informed us that we were grounded for the next few weeks and it was time for me to leave. All told, it wasn't that bad, but in the moment it was excruciating. Years later, she would tell me that night was the night her father fell in love with me. The average guy would have dropped her off and been on his way, but he respected the fact that I stood with her to face the consequences of our actions.

Aside from that incident, the summer of 1994 was largely uneventful, except for the KMEL Summer Jam concert. I went with Teo, who I'd known since fifth grade. We'd gone before together, but this year we were able to upgrade from lawn seats to assigned seats and backstage passes.

That was the day I decided to try marijuana for the first time. Many of friends were smokers and I was no stranger to its presence. It had never held any interest for me up until that moment. I'd done a lot of research on it and its effects so I knew what I was getting into; the days of Nancy Reagan's "Just Say No" campaign and the fear mongering of gateway drugs had long receded in light of my own analysis.

Teo hadn't offered me any because he knew I didn't smoke, so he was shocked when I asked for the pipe. Until that moment, I had never examined the substance before and was fascinated by it. This stuff was different than the weed I'd seen at the many summer festivals I'd attended growing up. Whereas that stuff looked brown and dry, this was highlighter green with little white hairs. It was also very sticky to the touch. I'm not sure what I expected it to look like, but this wasn't it. I calmly packed my first bowl and took a hit.

I didn't like the taste of smoke and ash. There was also a slightly sweet yet bitter aftertaste as well. I took another hit and soon forgot about what it tasted like. I forgot about almost anything else as the sensation over took me.

Whatever I liked about alcohol quickly paled in comparison to this. The feeling of floating in water was now a feeling of floating in space. The sun felt warmer and brighter and I felt light as air. The thing I loved most was that there was no nausea; just a tingling sensation that spread throughout my body. As I looked through crystal clear eyes at my surroundings, I couldn't help but feel the need to walk. I got up wordlessly from my seat and wondered around the venue; just taking it all in. I saw Da Brat backstage and thought she was fine.

And that is how my childhood ended. I knew not where I was headed, but I knew what I was leaving behind. I didn't know what would happen in Atlanta, and I didn't know what would happen with Dayna, but life was moving forward and I stood eagerly at the threshold to the rest of my life.

Year 18: Part 1 - The Dirty South

I hated Atlanta on sight. As soon as I stepped off the plane, I was enveloped by the sticky, humid air of a Georgian summer. I'd never felt anything like it in my life. The thickness of the air seemed to weigh me down and make every breath a chore. When I left the confines of air-conditioned corridors and stepped into the full force of the summer heat, I was sure I was going to pass out. This was not going to work. I needed to go back home.

Despite the dense, humid air, I was excited to see the place I would call home for the next year. As we exited the highway, my idyllic visions of a picturesque campus slowly receded, replaced with the sight of housing projects and urban blight. We drove about a mile before we came to a series of three-story buildings. We had arrived—the Morehouse plaque affixed to a brick retaining wall confirmed it.

Surely this had to be a mistake. This looked nothing like a college campus. Missing was the majestic buildings and grounds that connoted academia and sophistication. I had effectively moved from one hood to another hood, but with no sidewalks and worse weather.

Move-in day brought more unpleasant surprises. Remy,

Jabari, and myself were lucky enough to be roommates and granted one of the larger rooms—but the room was at best 200 square feet. The idea of sleeping on a bunk bed wasn't appealing, but being on the top bunk made it bearable.

The following weeks were filled with Morehouse's attempts to indoctrinate us. From spirit nights in oppressively hot tents, to mandatory convocations, they had a mold they were trying to conform us to. I didn't mind the mandates to have our "brother's back", the mantra that "being on time is to be late and being late is unacceptable" and the like; it was the rest of the Christian-based, deference to authority, and Southern ways of doing things that bothered me.

Almost immediately, we went about the business of becoming notorious. Our goal wasn't to be antagonistic for the sake of conflict, but we were quick to correct any offering of disrespect—real or perceived. From our walk, talk, dress, and especially our music, we made sure to represent who we were while enjoying the best parts of the new cultures we encountered.

As I ventured into the city, I found Atlanta to be the most racially segregated place I'd ever been. While I'd encountered variations of this on the liberal West Coast, the dividing line was more economic than ethnic. In California, if you could afford it, you could have it. This was not the feeling I received in Atlanta. Black people lived south of downtown and White people lived north, regardless of income. The lack of diversity, aside from black and white, was difficult to comprehend. I missed my Hispanic and Asian brothers and sisters and the energy they manifested.

I couldn't wait to get home. I hated the South and I missed

Dayna. We spoke nearly every day, but each passing week brought additional weight that was increasingly difficult to carry. The longer we were apart, the more difficult it was to maintain our love in the face of cold logistics. I missed her, but I was constantly enthralled with the sheer number and variety of women in close proximity.

The chaos of first semester, dropping my computer science major, and my heartache made being home for Christmas a welcome respite. I was mentally drained and I needed the downtime, but the situation with Dayna provided few opportunities to decompress. We weren't fighting, but there was a level of tension between us that made our interactions awkward and unrewarding. Despite the trials we had endured, I was still a novice regarding expressing my emotions and showing appreciation for her.

So it must have come as a shock to her when, after a few weeks back at school, I broke up with her. I'd had enough of the burning in my heart. I was mentally spent from my studies and the long-distance distraction. Maybe we could revisit this at some other time, but for now, I had to do me. We both vowed to be friends.

Eventually, I started dating an Atlanta native. Candace was a student at Spelman College and had a charming Southern accent. One night, Dayna asked if I had started dating and I admitted that I had. I'm sure it hurt her, but she seemed to accept that this would be part of our ultimate journey. What she didn't expect was needless detail I had the bright idea to add:

"She's everything I could have hoped for in a girl."

And with that, I squandered the goodwill that I had earned

back with Dayna over the previous year.

"Have a nice life!" she said and hung up the phone.

It wasn't too long before Candice and I would part ways. There wasn't anything wrong with us, but there was nothing right. To be honest, I was getting bored with her. As nice and beautiful as she was, we just didn't click. There was an increasing lack of warmth from her; warmth that I'd grown accustomed to being with Dayna. I knew I needed to get my girl back.

My first few phone calls ended quickly. She didn't want to hear anything I had to say. My persistence eventually resulted in a number of heartfelt conversations comprised primarily of me confessing some of my sins; chief among them being neglect and a lack of appreciation. Pieces of my pride and ego were gladly placed as a sacrifice on the altar of hope. All of this was in preparation for our pending vacation. Spring Break would be the key to bringing this thing home.

When I went home, I spent my entire break with her. If your name wasn't Dayna, you barely saw me. Whatever she wanted to do was fine by me. I was even willing to spend time at *Michael's* craft store, a place I loathed, just to reiterate my commitment to putting her first in my life. I'd earned this prison and I figured I'd only have to do all of this one time. She was worth it.

She waited until I returned to Atlanta to tell me that I'd wasted my time. She was tired of me overlooking her, hurting her, not appreciating her until I was in danger of losing her. As I listened in stunned silence, she ran through a long list of my transgressions.

"What about Spring Break?"

"I was just taking the attention you owed me."

And she was right. I did owe her, but so much more than she understood at that moment. I owed her the rest of my life. This was still the girl that loved me more than I knew I was worth.

Year 19: Part 1 - You Can't Go Home Again

The only thing on my mind during the summer of 1995 was getting Dayna back. The fact that she was now dating some guy named Michael would only add to the sweetness of the victory. I was invigorated by the challenge. I heard about all the ways he was better than me, but I had something he didn't: knowledge.

She was made for me and I was coming to reclaim what was mine. We were connected in ways no one else could ever understand. I actually felt bad for the guy. He had no idea what was about to happen to him. I never asked her to leave him. I never talked down on him. I felt no need to go out of my way to do anything; my opportunity would reveal itself.

I'd call occasionally to see how she was doing. I never stayed on the phone long; just long enough to touch base and keep it moving. The object wasn't to try and get her back in one fell swoop, but to make sure she felt my presence. She was my friend, after all. I still wanted to know she was happy and well, even if she was with someone else.

When the subject of us did come up, the consistent answer

was that I was an asshole. I'd had my shot and I never showed real appreciation for the magic that we had. No matter how much I wanted to argue the point, I knew she was right. Besides, she would say, it would never work with me living on the other side of the country. Long distance wasn't something she wanted to try anymore.

As the Dayna situation slowly unfolded, I spent the rest of my time hanging out with the guys and doing odd jobs around the city. I'd signed up with a job placement agency and they sent me out to all manner of jobs—the most consequential one being my placement with Sybase.

This was the first job I'd ever had that made me feel connected to the economy at large. I worked in the warehouse filling parts orders for the various databases and systems they manufactured and maintained. I was on my feet for hours on end, but with the right shoes and a CD player, it was actually kind of fun.

As I became more familiar with the products, I started to see patterns regarding which parts were required to be shipped in tandem. This insight allowed me to complete orders at an increasingly faster rate. It was like a game to me; could I beat my best times?

This effort wasn't lost on the warehouse foreman, Mr. Smith. He was a middle-aged black man who had been with the company for a number of years. He didn't favor me in any type of way, but one day he stopped me to tell me how well I was doing and how impressed he was with my work ethic.

Over the course of the summer, Mr. Smith would greet me when we saw each other, and he slowly got to know more about me. He commended me on my attendance at Morehouse College and my pursuit of a computer science degree. He learned that I wasn't happy with the program at Morehouse and probably gathered that I wasn't too thrilled with the South in general.

One day, he called me to his office. He said he wanted to share an opportunity with me. A good friend of his was recruiting for the business school at San Francisco State University with access to scholarship funds. He knew I was unhappy in Atlanta and wanted me to consider making a change in majors and schools. I asked for a few days to contemplate what was being offered.

In truth, I'd made the decision as soon as he offered the opportunity to me. I hated Atlanta and Morehouse was oversold. I knew how much money it was costing to continue there and the impact it was having on my mother. She was making it all work, but I wanted to remove myself as a concern for her. Most importantly, I saw an opportunity to remove the largest obstacle in the way of making Dayna and I work—the distance.

The news was a shock to Remy and Jabari. We had made a pact to take this journey together and I was dropping out. I think Remy understood though. The potential to repair my relationship with the love of my life was too important an opportunity to pass up. Besides, he wasn't the biggest fan of Atlanta and Morehouse either.

Dayna wasn't surprised at all. She knew that underneath my cautious exterior was a deep well of impulsivity. She also knew that I did it for her. She wasn't exactly pleased with the turn of events and the implications it had on her new relationship, but I knew the gesture wasn't lost on her. For years she'd asked for some show of my appreciation for what we had and what she meant to me and this was as big as it could get.

Everything was set up perfectly. I accepted the scholarship, enrolled at San Francisco State, and was finally in a position to pursue Dayna with renewed purpose. There was a bit of friction with my mother because she wasn't used to me being autonomous in my comings and goings, but that was no big deal. I was home and that's all that I wanted: the security and comfort of the familiar. So why did I have a sinking feeling in my stomach when Dayna called me to say that she had broken up with Michael?

Something about it felt wrong, and I could tell in her voice that she wasn't happy with herself. From all accounts, he was a decent guy that treated her with respect and appreciation, things that I'd always struggled with. He was polite and considerate, and I knew she really cared about him. To betray that kindness for selfish reasons was hurtful to him. She was becoming like me.

This is what I wanted, I told myself. Not quite like this, but I wasn't going to complain about the details. We'd take it slow, we promised. She needed time to heal and we needed to adjust to the changes in our dynamic. It all sounded fine to me; I had everything I wanted.

I was looking forward to my birthday. Even though we'd known each other for the past three years, I'd never had the opportunity to spend my birthday with my girl. Having a September birthday usually meant that it was buried in back to school activities, or in our case, missed opportunities. And while these things conspired to make my birthday somewhat of a nonevent for me, the anticipation of spending it with Dayna gave this birthday extra significance.

Answering her invitation of a birthday dinner at her house, she sat me at the dining room table and proceeded to bring me a number of dishes, all deliciously and meticulously prepared by her. Even though I prefer to cook for myself and my woman, I was enjoying the opportunity to be served. She was a good cook; rare for girls our age. Dayna was unusually quiet. Initially, I thought she was focusing on being a good hostess, but as the night progressed I sensed that something was bothering her. It wasn't until dinner was complete and I was thoroughly content that she plunged the proverbial knife into my heart:

"I'm breaking up with you."

I'd made her hurt a good guy that never did wrong by her. For a week she had wrestled with what she'd done, but there was no way to reconcile it. I was corrupt, and it was infecting her. And for that, she had to push me as far away as possible. No matter how much I protested, she remained firm. She was right; I was the bad guy.

I left that evening knowing that I would never see her again.

On top of this emotional upheaval, San Francisco State wasn't the place that I hoped it would be. The campus was beautiful with facilities that far outpaced what was available at Morehouse, but something was off. Gone were classes of no more than 28 people; replaced with auditoriums of 200 to 300 people. My largest class had nearly 1000 people.

Compounding my discomfort, I was one of less than a handful of black people in my science and business classes. Where I did find a number of black students were in the humanity and social science classes. It seemed as if everyone was studying to be a teacher, social worker, or find some deeper understanding of the African diaspora.

Why weren't more of us seeking expertise in the fields that would bring security and wealth to our families and our community at large? Sure, we needed social services and knowledge of our history, but we also needed economics.

For me, two paths became very clear to me. The first of little resistance: I could stay in Oakland and be comfortable. I could keep doing the same old things with the same old friends. I could surround myself with people who weren't as driven as me. The other path would require a shedding of all I'd ever known. I would have to give up my home and comfort, put distance between me and my friends, and pursue a future that was still just an idea. Success would not be guaranteed.

I knew that staying stagnant was no longer an option. I had to keep moving forward. That meant I had to move back to Atlanta and Morehouse.

When I broke the news to my mother, she wasn't pleased. To her, I had made my decision and the lives in the family had been adjusted to accommodate the new reality. More importantly, I had made a decision and I would have to live with it. I tried to explain the rationale for my change of heart, but she didn't want to hear it. The new school year was barely a month old and she was moving on with her life.

I sunk deeper and deeper into depression. Between the stress at home, trying to maintain a scholarship at an institution I didn't want to attend, and the loss of my girl, I couldn't find much to be happy about. As the days and weeks passed, I looked for a way out. Although I had a job and was productive with my time, I began to drink and smoke weed with increased frequency. I had only one burning desire:

GET THE HELL OUT OF OAKLAND.

The only thing holding me back was my lack of funds. A year's tuition and board at Morehouse cost $16,000 and I had nothing to my name. If you add in incidentals, I figured I needed about $20,000 to get through the year. I could work out the details later, I imagined, but how to obtain that first $20,000?

As a bitter silence enveloped my home, my mind was filled with a burning desire to escape. I could barely pay attention in class due to searing pressure of this all-consuming need. During one of those quietly desperate moments, with little to lose and my mind fixated on making the money I needed, my eye wondered around the room and settled on the bulletin board near the door. As I looked over the various postings, I saw it. Staring back at me was the answer to my prayers: I could earn $25,000 on a fishing boat in Alaska.

Year 19: Part 2 - Stay on the Path; Ask for Direction

I knew Alaska was a drastic decision, but fear couldn't be a reason not to step into the batter's box and take my swing at life. Staying in Oakland might as well have been the end of this story, and that wasn't good enough for me.

It took me a few days to sit with this decision before I broke the news to my mother. I didn't ask her opinion or feelings on the matter; I simply informed her of my decision. It wasn't until that moment that it dawned on her that this thing in my heart was bigger than buyer's remorse.

My desire to leave wasn't a desire to run away, but a decision to run towards something bigger. She knew from the look in my eye that I was set on my new course and that she had a decision to make: would she stand aside and let me risk life and limb in the Bearing Sea or would she help her only son?

Another day or so passed before my mother gave me her reply—she had decided to help. We talked more about why I wanted to leave and what I wanted for my life. I would suffocate if I stayed home. I couldn't be a guy that left home for a year, came back and just became an older version of who I was in high school. For me, that would be a failure and a waste of life. I was willing to sacrifice it all on a fishing boat in Alaska if it meant a way out.

Perhaps I hadn't been as articulate as I needed to be in expressing my need before, but it was a real need. Sure, I was heartbroken over Dayna, but that was a sign, not a cause. My life had to be more than pining after some girl I'd once dated in high school. Be it Alaska or Atlanta, I was leaving.

She only asked one concession of me—complete this full year at San Francisco State. I had made a decision and she wanted me to see it through. The additional semester would also allow her time to gather the resources to make the move back to Atlanta possible. Despite my desire to leave immediately, I knew she was right.

In the long term, this was a win. I had a clear path forward that wouldn't require me to risk life and limb in some obscure corner of the Earth. It was even good in the short-term, as it brought peace to conflicts which had grown with my mother since my return home. Despite these wins, however, I was already further down the path of depression and apathy than I realized.

The most insidious aspect of depression is that you don't realize you're in its grasp until the grip is firm. I was aware of my depression, but I didn't understand the full extent of it because I was either high or drunk on a daily basis. More often than not, it was a combination of the two. And who would notice such a thing when you're high functioning? I was doing as well as I'd ever done in school and I had a part time job. I was checking all of the right boxes.

With my mother finally agreeing to help me get back to Atlanta, I only had to survive the rest of the school year. I won't even say that I was having a bad time, because I was actually having a ball. I'd go to school for class, work a few hours in the afternoon, meet up with the fellas to listen to music, play video games, and all the assorted things a normal college student would do. I even had rules for my inebriation:

1. Don't get high or drunk when you're feeling sad.
2. Never drink or smoke alone; that's addict behavior.
3. Be careful of the thoughts you bring into your inebriation.

The problem was that none of this left room for self-reflection. Some might consider this a minor thing, but reflection and self-analysis were the weapons I'd used to cut through the binds of poverty and self-doubt. As long as I was checking my boxes, I thought I was all right. As the seasons changed and the school year progressed, I continued to tell myself these lies. The lubrication of vice made them easier to swallow.

I felt untouchable. You couldn't tell me I wasn't winning. In response to my renewed dedication and my pending need of transportation in Atlanta, my mother found a way to buy me a new 1996 Mustang. I never understood how she did it, but it was just another example of my mother making a way when there seemed to be none. She was amazing that way.

There was a constant, fiery sensation in my chest yearning to break free and burn down all obstacles in my path. There was a larger plan at work that I wasn't quite grasping, however. Not in a religious sense, mind you, but on a spiritual level.

I wasn't quite one with the universe, but I was becoming more aware of the threads that spread and connected my actions to the environment around me. Or maybe I was just really high all the time. Something was changing, though.

It was late one evening when I began to gain a greater sense of clarity. I was hanging with my friends Brian and JaDaun. Hungry and bored, someone mentioned Taco Bell and we managed to scrape ten dollars together.

The lobby was closed, only the drive-thru was open, and we were the only people out except for a guy arguing with the cashier (on foot in front of the take-out window). We placed our order over the intercom and drove to the window to pay when the guy walked up to the driver's window. It was Oakland, late at night, and the guy looked a step or two above homeless status. I was wary, but I opened the window to hear what he had to say, because fear and disrespect were known to escalate a benign encounter into a full-blown situation.

Having our attention, he went into a story about how he just got off work and was hungry, but they wouldn't serve him without a car. He pleaded with me to make the order for him, assuring me he had the money to pay. Still looking for the angle, I thought about it for a second or so, before asking to verify the money. He slipped a bill in my hand and as I unfolded it, I realized it was a hundred-dollar bill.

A hundred dollars?!

I hit the gas.

"WAIT! WAIT! COME BACK!!!!"

The mood in the minivan was joyous. Ten minutes before, we had a hard time scraping together ten dollars and now we had ten times that amount. Given our windfall, we decided to upgrade to the authentic Mexican restaurant further down the street. And while we were at it, a trip to deep East Oakland to get a bag of weed from a corner dealer would be the perfect ribbon on the escapade.

It wasn't until I was back home, high, full and rested, that I reflected on the events of the evening; more specifically, the scream that man gave as I robbed him. It wasn't a scream of anger or shock, but one of desperation.

Here was a man that was obviously having a tough time and only wanted something to eat. He was tired and beat down from whatever manual labor he had secured for that day—wages in hand. He'd probably been formulating a plan to have that money feed him all week; maybe even a family. And I robbed him for the thrill of it—just because I could.

I'd been stealing for nearly half my life at that point. If I could find a way to take it, it was mine to have. It had always been about the thrill, but not that night. I was ashamed and disgusted. I was the guy preying on someone else's lack of power for my own thrill; to get fat and high. That night that I made a promise to myself: I would never take advantage of anyone else ever again.

I spent the rest of the summer focusing on things I enjoyed: making money and getting high. People will tell you that smoking weed kills your ambition, but I had three jobs that summer. I worked at a sporting goods store, as a summer camp counselor, and did janitorial work in downtown Oakland with a number of my friends.

I was a model young man as far as anyone was concerned, so I felt empowered to do whatever I wanted. That included smoking as much as I wanted, as well as growing a very healthy marijuana plant of my own.

When the summer ended, I packed my car for the cross-country drive back to school. There wasn't a moment's hesitation about bringing my carefully cultivated weed plant. My friends urged me to leave it behind, but the idea of bringing a self-sustaining source of high-grade marijuana to Atlanta was too enticing. With a few weeks left to mature, I packed the potted plant in the back seat of my car with my other belongings, covered by a sheet to shield from prying eyes.

In August, I departed for Atlanta, along with JaDaun and his girlfriend, Miesha. The first leg of the trip was a short drive to Los Angeles. We could have driven further, but we wanted to see an old friend from high school who had gotten married and relocated. We had a good time that evening, but they were also concerned with the plant in the back of the car.

"I got this!" I said with confidence. "You guys worry too much. I have it all figured out."

We left Los Angeles on I-10 early the next morning to beat the traffic out of town. My bright red Mustang gleamed in the desert sun. My black Adidas track suit and black driving gloves only added to my sense of cool.

Instead of staying on the main interstate, I saw on the map what appeared to be a shortcut through the mountains just east of Phoenix. We could cut about two hours off the time to our next stop.

JaDaun wasn't thrilled with the idea, but there wasn't much protest from either of them. It wasn't until we were a good thirty miles or so down the alternate route that my bright idea began to lose some of its luster: the interstate transitioned to a state highway that ran through multiple small towns with the requisite lower speed limits. I tried to make up lost time by pushing the limits of the posted speed.

I barely acknowledged the rapidly approaching yellow traffic light in Globe, AZ., as I sped through the intersection. I was intent on making up the time my questionable decision seemed to be losing us. The lights of a patrol car entered the highway but I was in denial.

If I can get around the next bend, I won't have to worry about it, I thought.

As I downshifted into second gear and the car accelerated, I could sense the fear and anxiety from my friends.

What am I doing? I thought.

I pulled off the highway into the nearest lot and waited for the officer.

When the officer finally arrived, he exited his patrol car with his firearm drawn.

"Driver, get out of the car!"

Despite the hurricane surrounding me, I was exceptionally calm. As I got out of the car, closed the door, and backed up towards him, I was in complete control. He must have sensed my energy, because he immediately put his firearm away as JaDaun and Miesha exited the car and joined us. She left the car door open, and I was immediately annoyed.

"Why didn't you pull over? Looks to me like you were attempting to flee."

"Dude, I didn't see you and when I did, I stopped and waited for you."

By this time, I felt the situation was under control. The arrival of another patrol car wasn't enough to break my calm either. The opened passenger door was a detail that I still wasn't pleased about.

"We're three black kids away from home. We didn't know what was going to happen!" Miesha said.

Bringing up the race card never helps when dealing with cops. Racist or not, it would just serve to irritate the authorities.

I heard the cop say something about being part Native American, irritation heavy in his voice. I was too busy watching the second officer inspect the outside of my car, duck his head into the still open passenger door, and peek under the sheet covering my marijuana plant.

Everything moved rapidly after that. I took responsibility for everything in the car and was placed under arrest. A quick search of everyone's person revealed that Miesha had a small bag of marijuana in her purse and she was arrested as well. JaDaun was clean so he was free to go.

"Listen…" the officer said, "this isn't going to be that bad. We'll take you down, get you arraigned, and you can post bail or bond. Before we go, is there anything else I ought to know?"

"Well, uh…yeah. There's an unloaded .25 semi-automatic handgun in the trunk under all my stuff. I found it."

The gun wasn't mine; I was returning it to a friend who had left it in California. I knew it wasn't against the law to be in possession of a gun, but having a gun in proximity to a controlled substance was problematic.

The officer just looked at me for a second, sizing me up. I think he really liked me and knew I was a good kid, because he had a look of disappointment on his face.

"You better hope that gun doesn't have a body on it."

Year 19: Part 3 - Pride Only Hurts

As the deputy escorted me to my cell, I was still confident that I could figure a way out of this mess. I figured it would take no longer than a day or so to be arraigned and released; a timeline easily explainable for a cross country road trip. That is, of course, if JaDaun and Miesha kept their word to not call my mother. With such a minor amount of marijuana, I couldn't have been looking at anything more than a fine or so. I just needed to be cool and bide my time.

There was a surprising amount of dullness to the jail. Aside from the bland colors of concrete and steel, the repetitive nature of the daily schedule slowed the passage of time. Numbness weighed on the mood of everything. It was as if this place existed in another dimension—an exceedingly boring one. The recesses of my mind called to me with invitations of a more vibrant existence and I happy retreated into them.

I was arrested on a Friday and wouldn't see the judge until the following Monday. Aside from my cellmate, I had little interaction with anyone. I was aware that I was the only black man in the cell block; the rest being a mix of Mexicans, Native Americans, and Whites. I locked everything away in my mind, only projecting a blank slate to the other men on the cell block. I had no friends and I wasn't looking for any. I was content to be left alone, but was ready to introduce them to "East Oakland" if needed.

I guess this didn't sit well with the other men on the cell block, because around the second afternoon I received a visitor in the guise of a 300lbs Native American. As he entered uninvited into my cell, I sat up on my bunk.

This is the test, I thought. *If we have to take that ass whipping, so be it....but we won't be a punk!*

I tuned out the sound of his voice as he began to speak to me. I was intensely focused on attempting to read his body language. I nodded and provided the setup phrases for him to continue saying whatever he had to say. His mannerisms remained relaxed as he queried about my presence in the jail.

I provided that I was from California and was being held on a gun and marijuana charge; things he probably already knew. And that was it. He had seen me around and wanted to make sure I was alright. As he left, he said to let him know if I needed anything. I thanked him, but told him I'd be alright.

"Don't be a stranger," he replied. "You don't have to stay in your cell all the time. Everyone here is cool. Maybe we can play cards later."

After lunch, I hung out in the main area instead of going back to my cell. I sat at the end of a table casually observing the moments of my neighbors. There were two factions on the block. The cells in the back block were populated by white guys, while cells in the front of the block were populated by everyone else. I initiated no contact, but offered head nods to anyone that happened to catch my eye. It was a passively aggressive stance to show I was neither intimidated by their presence nor eager to make contact. I simply was; the true embodiment of a rock.

Despite the apparent segregation within the tier, there seemed to be no animosity between anyone. The guys were just hanging out but preferred to bunk "with their own kind." Somehow or another I found myself playing spades with Bear, my cell mate, and a white guy that was very proud of the fact of his skin color. He even had a tattoo over his heart that said "101% White" to prove it. I later learned the reason for the peaceful coexistence: everyone in the cell block either had only a few months on their sentence or were waiting to see a judge. There was no incentive to cause problems that could result in added complications to one's case.

Once Monday came, I waited to be transported to the courthouse. The shackles against my bare ankles chafed as I shuffled with my peers. The length of the binding chain was slightly shorter than a natural stride, but even that amount of movement was increasingly irritating as the metal scraped against my bare flesh. I slowed to a slight shuffle to avoid any unnecessary movement. It's these small indignities that are the real punishment, I realized.

I waited patiently until it was my time to be arraigned. The mundaneness of the affair was immediately punctured as the judge read the list of charges against me: felony evasion, felony possession of marijuana, and criminal possession of a firearm.

My minor worries bloomed into full blown concern. My hopes had been pinned on the fact that I had a minor amount of contraband. The plant hadn't even bloomed and was essentially a bunch of twigs and leaves. I assumed everything would be confiscated and I would be released. They were even including the weight of the dirt in their calculations. There was no way I was going to talk my way out of this.

Assessing the totality of my situation, I was forced to concede that I'd finally found myself in a situation that I couldn't talk my way out of. There was no amount of reasoning or bargaining that was going to make it better. I was looking at years in prison and only had myself to blame. The more I contemplated my predicament, my feeling of shame threatened to overtake me.

Despite all of my hard work and the sacrifices of others on my behalf, I had thrown it all away. I'd fallen into the trap that was laid decades prior to my existence. The only thing that would be remembered of me was that I just another young black man caught in the web of crime, drugs, and prison. For all of my bravado and boasts that I would break the rules and transcend my environment, I was just another nigga.

With my ego humbled, I worked up the courage to do the first thing I should have done but was the thing that frightened me most: I called my mother.

"Where are you?" she asked.

"I'm in jail, Mama."

I made multiple calls to coordinate information with my mother. The deputies were extremely gracious in letting me use the office phone. They could have been assholes about it and made me call collect, but they didn't.

I slept well that evening. I knew my mother was working on the problem and that she would have me out sooner than later. And when I awoke the next morning, I was released without having to post bail or bond.

As soon as I was out, I called my mother. She quickly vetoed my ideas of continuing my trip. Her explicit instructions were to get JaDaun to the nearest Greyhound bus station and to bring Miesha and myself home. There was no room for debate.

I made it home without incident to my mother's embrace. She wasn't angry, just disappointed and relieved. Thankfully, I hadn't jeopardized our plan to send me back to Atlanta, but she wanted me home to collect myself. Airline tickets were purchased for both me and Miesha to fly to Atlanta. For reasons unknown to me, she bought a ticket for Miesha. Miesha wasn't her child nor had pressing business in Atlanta, but my mother understood that this young lady needed a new start.

I needed a new start as well, but this wasn't a matter of location. I shed a fair number of tears thinking about what my fate would be. I was looking at a year in jail and the permanent stain of a felony on my record. A year in jail was bad enough, but the lifelong tag of being a convicted felon worried me. My career prospects would be severely restricted, as well as my civil rights. I would be a second-class citizen with little to no recourse.

But this was the bed I had made. There were no time machines to take me back to correct this error in judgment. I was going to have to live with it. Most importantly, I was going to have to grow up and accept what my life could possibly be. And in that acceptance, I found peace. I would be okay as long as I kept my head up and my eyes forward.

The first six weeks of school passed quickly as I awaited my court date in Arizona. Despite my initial fears of what court would hold, there were positive signs that this entire ordeal might be managed with little disruption to my normal life. This was, after all, my first offense. I was able to gather numerous character witness that penned letters on my behalf. Nothing was promised, but I was feeling hopeful.

I flew to Los Angeles to meet my mother on a Sunday afternoon in October. After an afternoon's drive and an evening spent on the eastern fringes of Phoenix, my mother and I awoke to the most beautiful sky I'd ever seen. The clouds were like fluffy cotton balls aligned in perfect perpendicular rows from horizon to horizon. The sun rose over the eastern mountains, casting rays of crimson, pink, orange, and a spectrum of other colors I couldn't describe.

We stood motionless, staring in wonder at this tapestry of natural beauty. Any lingering fear I had melted away in the face of this awesome view. As long as there was beauty like this in the world, there would always be a reason to wake up and maximize the opportunities available.

When we arrived at the courthouse to meet with my attorney, she'd already crafted a reasonably fair plea agreement. The conditions of the deal were as follows:

1. Plead guilty to felony possession of marijuana.
2. Pay a fine of $1000.
3. Accept probation of 12 months.
4. 40 hours of community service (to be completed in Georgia).
5. The charges of firearm possession and felony evasion would be waived.
6. Upon successful completion of probation, the felony would be downgraded to misdemeanor possession.

This was my "get out of jail (almost) free" card. Sure, I had to pay $1000 and I'd have to do some crap community service, but those were minor inconveniences to not be a felon. It wasn't lost on me that a lot of people didn't get deals like this. The entire ordeal, centered on a naturally occurring plant that causes little to no harm for its users, was an encroachment of natural rights. Despite my philosophical objection, I was happy to accept the slap on the wrist with my future intact.

Year 22: Speak Up
So They Can Hear You

I spent the next three years creating a future for myself. I focused my studies on Finance with an Economics minor and discovered a real passion to understand the information, instead of just learning to pass tests.

In these years, Dayna and I reconnected and tried to have a relationship again. She'd completed her associate's degree at San Francisco City College and was finishing her marketing degree at Hayward State University working as a resident's assistant. The state of our relationship was OK, but long distance added additional stressors that we still weren't quite able to get beyond.

I drove home from Atlanta that Christmas and quickly made my way to the campus to spend the night with her. Our greeting was warm, and we brought take-out back to her room. I was impressed with where she was in her life. Finally living on her own, I saw a growing strength and confidence in her. While those characteristics were always there, being on her own had allowed her to spread her wings just a little wider.

We talked about our various plans for the following year and what that could mean for us. The distance was starting to take its toll again, but we were determined to see this through. My most pressing concern was finding work as soon as I graduated. I would be just shy of my 23rd birthday and it was time for me to let go of my mother's apron strings.

Dayna, on the other hand, had another year to go because she decided to add a Spanish major to accompany her business degree. She was contemplating spending a year in Mexico to solidify her fluency. I encouraged her plans but suggested she rethink going to Mexico.

"Why did you choose Mexico?"

"I don't know. There are pictures of Mexico all over the Spanish department. And you know how much I love Mexican food."

"Seems to me that if you want to study Spanish, you should go to the source. You should go to Spain. Or that's what I would do. They use that other form of Spanish that Mexicans don't use too."

"Vosotros?"

"Yeah, that one. But whatever, that's just me."

I left early the next morning. I kissed Dayna goodbye and told her I would see her later. After spending half the day working my way through a list of people I'd promised to visit during vacation, I connected with Brian.

We met up with our friends, smoking, drinking, and hanging around town. At one point in the middle of the night, Brian and I found ourselves stopped on the side of the road. For years he'd been one of my closest friends and I greatly appreciated his counsel.

We stood on the side of that road, enjoying the cool

California morning and talking about our lives. He'd had a daughter the same month of the Arizona incident, and his life was much different than mine. We talked about our hopes, dreams, fears, and the journey we'd made thus far. We talked about our failures and we talked about love.

He talked to me about the love he had for his daughter and the clarity of purpose she provided for him. The more he talked, the more I listened to him. And the more I listened to him, the clearer my purpose became. I was wasting my life, not being true to who I was. My education was fine and my career prospects looked promising, but there was nothing that really sparked my passion except one thing: my love for Dayna.

I understand then, on the side of that road, just what a fool I'd been the past six years. I had the perfect woman—a woman who loved me despite my faults and shortcomings. A woman who had proven time and again that she had my best interests in mind. She was the woman I'd always dreamed of and I had never shown enough appreciation. There were no words to tell her how I felt, but I'd used too few until that moment.

"Dude, you just helped me see everything. I have to go. I'm wasting time here in the streets when I could be with Dayna. I love that girl, man. Fuck, I'm going to marry her! No better time to start the rest of my life than right now."

"I feel you, dude. Go get it then!" I left him there and headed straight to Dayna's.

I had a surge of exhilaration as I drove down the street and dialed her number to let her know I was on my way. It was 3 o'clock in the morning, so it rang several times before she finally answered.

"Hello?" Her voice crackled, heavy with sleep and a note of irritation.

"Hey," I said, smiling at the sleep in her voice, "I'm on my way over." I couldn't wait to see her face.

"Where have you been all day?"

"I've been out with B. I really need to talk to you."

"And you couldn't call me?" The note of irritation was more pronounced this time.

"I was out visiting with everyone. I'm on my way to you, though. We really need to talk."

"I don't feel like talking right now…"

This wasn't how this was supposed to go.

I tried to make her understand how important it was that I talk to her right now, but she didn't seem to understand that she was spoiling the moment.

"I don't want to see you now."

She was fully awake at that point. The irritation I'd heard earlier was gone. In its place was anger.

"So when can I see you?"

"I don't know…later this week. Go hang with your boys."

Silence ensued.

"So you really don't want me to come over?" I asked incredulously.

"Just go home."

She hung up the phone, leaving me stunned. Why was she always so emotional? She had ruined the most perfect beginning to the rest of our lives.

It took her four days to decide she wanted to see me. I was nervous, but my opportunity to present my heart to her was here and I was eager to grab the opportunity.

"I can't do this anymore," she said as soon as we sat down to talk.

"What do you mean, 'you can't do this'?" The panic was beginning to rise in the back of my throat. I knew what she meant, but I didn't want to believe it, not when we were on the cusp of something special.

"I don't want to be with you. I'm tired, Roc. Tired of always being second to everything else in your life!"

"But that's what I've been trying to say to you all week!" I pleaded. "I love you and I know that I haven't been good about saying that, but I'm saying it now. I know what you need and I want to be that man for you. I've always loved you with everything that I have, and I want to marry you and make a family with you."

"It's too late," she said, deadpan.

"Why aren't you listening to me?" The corners of my eyes began to burn from the salty tears that threatened to spill onto my face.

Her eyes flashing cold and hard, she raised her voice slightly to make sure there was no mistaking her intentions.

"I DON'T LOVE YOU!" she said with contempt.

Humiliated, I stared at her for a brief second before I left.

Fuck her, I thought. If she was too damn proud to see what I was presenting, then she wasn't the one for me. I probably wasn't coming home when I finished school anyway. I had a number of interviews already lined up and my future looked bright. *Who really ends up with their high school sweetheart anyway?*

I was determined to enjoy the rest of my vacation, so a few

days later some of the guys and I decided to go to a club in Jack London Square. Far from depressed, I was looking forward to what life would bring next. I wouldn't say I was looking for a girl, but I was in the mood for my next adventure.

As it happens, adventure was on the dance floor of the club that evening in the guise of a pretty young girl. Her slender build made her 5'5" frame seem long and lithe. She was alone, but more than a few tried to grab her attention. The way she moved had nearly every man in the club fixated on her. She was sex in human form.

I'm not one to stand in line to talk to any chick, so I didn't bother to make a move. There were too many dudes vying for her attention and I wasn't about to make myself random guy #8. It wasn't until after the club closed that I saw an opportunity. She was about a half block away; walking up the street with a girlfriend of hers. I quickly caught up with them and made my move.

"Excuse me, but you look like the type of girl I could write poetry for." It was a winning line, judging by the bright smile she gave me.

"You write poetry?" she asked sweetly.

"I do...when I'm inspired," I said knowingly.

And with that, Kizzy was mine. I picked her up the next evening and took her to Skates on the Bay for drinks and dinner.

She grew up in Montana, a bi-racial girl in an all-white family. Her father met her mother passing through town for a motorcycle convention. She had moved around a bit growing up, the results of a poor upbringing complete with stints in various trailer parks.

She hadn't been in Oakland long. She'd just recently moved from Las Vegas where she'd been a dancer. In spite of everything, she had a heart of gold. Sure, she had broken bits, but who didn't? She wanted more than what life had given her thus far. And she was exactly what I was looking for then: cheerful fun, and sexy. What wasn't to like?

Returning to school, I refocused my thoughts on my pending graduation and need for a job. For me, college was a means to a more sustainable career. I needed to generate a living income, because in six months I would be on my own.

I didn't know much about Enron when I applied; I was just curious. Why was an energy company seeking finance majors? I conducted a cursory review of their online company profile, but there is only so much information you can gather from public relation profiles.

When I went for my interview, it was more because of my curiosity than interest. I probably asked more questions of them than they asked of me. This must have been an unconventional and refreshing attitude, because the recruiter wanted me to stay an additional hour to talk to his partner.

I shouldn't have been surprised when an offer was extended to attend the final recruiting round in Houston, but I was. I didn't think I came off particularly well, but they seemed to like it and I was getting an all-expense paid trip to Houston, so it was a win.

It wasn't until I arrived in Houston that I began to get nervous. This was one of the fastest growing companies in the country with a global reach. At the time, they were a Fortune 50 company with an insane growth trajectory given the rapid deregulation of energy markets around the world.

At cocktail hour, the full weight of the opportunity became apparent to me. These people were serious. There was information about all the various interests they were involved in from energy transportation to future trading in energy contracts and weather. They were recruiting students from high profile schools across North America including Harvard, McGill, University of Texas, and many others.

As I placed my name tag on my chest with Morehouse College underscoring my name, I felt outgunned. These kids were the heavy hitters. Their schools had deeper resources and they most likely came from more affluent families and communities. They'd been trained for this moment their entire lives. And here was I: the only black guy in the room, from a small school that few had heard of, from a city that most people feared. How was I supposed to compete with these guys?

And then it hit me: I wasn't here to compete; *I* was the competition.

I was the kid that overcame the pitfalls of society to be standing in this room. I'd dodged the bullets, figuratively and literally, to make it to this point in the game. I'd had to scrap and scrape, make unconventional alliances, and cut new paths. Their schools might be bigger, but 1+1=2 everywhere. I wasn't in the room with Harvard; Harvard was in the room with me!

When I received a formal offer of employment a few weeks later, I wasn't surprised. The offer of $36,000, a signing bonus of $4,000, and stock options was the cake—moving Kizzy in with me was the icing.

Graduation came on a warm May day as I listened to Oprah

Winfrey give our commencement speech. There were times that my mother thought she would never see this day. For too many years, my effort was subpar and my attitude was worse. I recognized that there were also financial hurdles she had to navigate to make this day happen—to walk across the stage was the best gift I could give my parents. I knew the future would be whatever I could forge it into—starting with the walk across the stage to accept my degree.

Even learning that my father's mother decided not to come to another graduation wasn't enough to dampen my spirits. Despite my mother having purchased a ticket for her, and only giving us a few days' notice, she offered no other explanation for her absence.

I understood that my name was not the easiest to pronounce, so I handed the announcer a cue card with a phonetic pronunciation guide. Despite these cues, he still butchered it.

My mother had paid far too much money to not hear my name said correctly. She deserved to hear my name associated with the best, instead of all the times she'd heard it in reference to something bad. So I backtracked across the stage to the announcer, relieved him of his microphone, and presented myself:

"RAHMAAN HUSSEIN MWONGOZI—thank you very much!"

Year 23: Houston, We Have A Problem

I left Atlanta within a month of graduation. Enron gave us the option of a June or September start, and I saw no reason to delay—that would be the equivalent of turning down $9,000. There wasn't a chance in hell I'd leave that much money on the table.

Kizzy didn't have as smooth as a transition. When she'd moved to Atlanta, she was able to transfer her job at Nordstrom's—but there was no Nordstrom's in Houston at that time. She was unemployed, which put a damper on our new life, but I was determined to make my way.

It didn't take long for me to develop two distinct groups of friends: the first year analysts, like me, and the older associates. To those of us in our first year, the associates seemed old as hell—even though they were probably in their mid-twenties. But they were several years into their careers and seemed to have it all figured out. I blended easily between the two groups—neither having any interaction with the other. It didn't escape my attention that the first group was completely white and the second was all black.

There was no racial or ethnic strife, despite the obvious separation. The divergence was due more to the stages of everyone's career and the school networks that everyone had a prior allegiance to—HBCUs versus all other schools.

Until I moved to Houston, I didn't have white friends past elementary school. My high school had been extremely diverse. And while I was cool with a lot of different types of people, there was very little socializing after hours. This was just an extension of the sorting that occurred after elementary school. Going to an HBCU only compounded this dynamic for me.

The guys I met were all cool dudes. We were a diverse group: a few from Canada, one from Colorado, some from Texas, and me. One of the Texans was extremely effeminate and we suspected he was in denial about being gay. We teased him about it often, but always that he should just come out. He was our guy and it was all good if he was, we just wanted him to drop the pretenses with us.

As varied as we were, we had all the important things in common: love of girls, football, beer, and weed. We spent many weekends in pursuit of all of these over Tex-Mex and barbeque. Through them, I met a wider network of people that I may not have had relations with. At the end of the day, we were all just young men on the same journey trying to make our way in the world.

As much as they were able to learn from me about my experiences in this world, I was able to learn an equal amount from them. For example, I was shocked that my Canadian friends were constantly on edge about their immigration status. I thought Canada was, more or less, figuratively considered a suburb of the United States and their citizens were able to cross the border at will. Who'd ever heard of a Canadian being hounded by immigration authorities? I assumed that was reserved for Mexicans and other brown people.

The relationships I made with the HBCU crew were not much different than those in high school. Though we were all from different parts of the country, we viewed each other as brothers and sisters of the greater African diaspora and all that encompassed. We were of the same tribe tasked with creating more space for people like us in corporate America.

Of all the people I met, Reggie and I became the closest. We were near the same age, had similar tastes in music, and our personalities were natural compliments. Reggie was a summer intern entering his senior year of undergrad. He was what we called a face man.

He was a handsome guy with an abundance of charisma and an endless amount of patience for the chase of girls. Sometimes, however, he had far more patience for them than I thought they deserved. No one embodied this dynamic more than when he was dating Ehren.

Ehren was an intern entering her senior year at Spelman College. Originally from Birmingham, Alabama, she had a Southern belle persona that grated on me. She acted as if she were the princess of the ball. It wasn't uncommon for us to end up arguing about the most insignificant things. I thought she was a spoiled brat giving my guy unnecessary attitude while she thought I was a jerk.

Despite the social gains I was making at work, fissures began to appear in my relationship with Kizzy. I imagine it was difficult for her to watch all of this from the sidelines. I tried to include her, and there were occasions when she would join at various functions, but those times seemed to agitate the situation. We all had our careers and education as common bonds while she didn't.

She was insecure, but I found it hard to be sensitive to that. It was up to her to find her path forward either in a career or continuing her education. Increasingly, I was regretting my decision to bring her to Houston with me. Her issues were becoming too much to bear, and I had my own issues to deal with.

Of all the possible rotations I could have been assigned to, I was sent to pipeline operations. I knew there was a problem when my new manager Stephanie told me she didn't know why I was there. She hadn't requested a new analyst and had no idea what project she could assign me to.

When I brought this issue to the rotation management team, they could only provide vague answers to my questions. No one knew anything about anything. The lack of transparency was troubling. I resolved to make the best out of the situation by enrolling in a number of available training classes.

As I completed more classes, however, I found the underlying principles to be troubling. Subjects such as managed energy service, where we managed energy savings for profit, made perfect sense. The class on energy derivatives was also easily understood, as energy sources such as natural gas and electricity generation were closely related. It wasn't until I attended my first class on weather derivatives that I began to question the knowledge base I was acquiring.

Weather derivatives were a series of options sold to customers with opposing views of meteorological events. We were given an example in class to better illustrate how they worked.

For the month of April, an ice cream maker needs at least 20 days above 75 degrees to make a profit. Achieving less than these minimums, they lose money. To offset this risk, they buy a weather derivative from Enron as insurance and pay premiums.

For the same month, a hot chocolate vendor needs at least 20 days below 75 degrees to make a profit. To offset their risk, they buy a weather derivative from Enron as insurance and pay premiums.

Theoretically, the premiums of each customer offset the insurance payout to the other while Enron collects a transaction and management fee.

The room remained silent as we let this knowledge sink in. It made perfect sense when explained in a specific way, but something about the entire enterprise didn't add up.

"So it's a bet?" someone chimed in. "And we're the middle man?"

"Exactly!" exclaimed the instructor, proud that his pupils were learning.

The scene from *Trading Places,* where the Dukes are explaining the business to Eddie Murphy, popped into my head. We were just a bunch of bookies.

"But what happens if you can't find a trading partner?" someone else asked.

"There's always another partner," the instructor assured us.

As entertaining and useful as these classes were, however, Stephanie had a problem with me attending them. She didn't want her analyst away for multiple days at a time. The fact that I had very little work seemed to escape her.

I watched my friends' careers progress, while I dealt with growing animosity towards me from my manager. The pressure was hard to take, and to top it off, I'd been feeling ill for several weeks. I was increasingly fatigued, and had trouble keeping food down when I was able to generate an appetite. I was sure the adjustment to the heat and humidity was the cause. Atlanta had been hot, but the Gulf weather was something else entirely.

It wasn't until I passed out in the middle of a staff meeting that I knew it was serious. One minute I was listening to the discussion and the next I woke up, dizzy and disoriented.

"Rahmaan, are you ok?" the division head asked as I tried to get my bearings. Everyone looked concerned—Stephanie's face only showed anger.

"I'm fine," I said, trying to minimize the situation.

I wasn't fine, however. My vision was blurred and I was working as hard as I could to maintain consciousness as the shadows at the periphery of my sight threatened to close in on me. The next morning, I sat in the doctor's office, drinking some high glucose concoction and having a slew of tests done.

"The good news is that you're fine," the doctor said. "While we didn't find anything serious, your tests indicate that you may have a slightly overactive thyroid gland."

In spite of the minor implications, I was still concerned about everything I'd been dealing with. I probed for a more definitive answer to my ongoing issues. We discussed my stress level and work habits, as well as my eating habits. I told him about my aversion to food but he assured me that there would be no long term effects if I made sure to pay closer attention to my diet.

I was relieved all would be okay with my health, but unfortunately, I still had to deal with the professional implications of what had occurred. As soon as I returned to the office, I let Stephanie know what the doctor had said. She responded to this information with a slight nod and pursed lips; my transfer out of her department would be finalized shortly thereafter.

I increasingly spent larger portions of my day in the recruiting office. Although I had access to a desk and computer to facilitate my job search, those activities didn't require much time. An hour or so was enough to stay abreast of all new job openings and to submit resumes. Without normal constraints on my time, I grew closer to a recruiter named George.

George was the head recruiter for a number of schools, including most of the HBCUs. In hindsight it was odd that he liked having me around to help him plan and execute recruiting trips. Given my ongoing conflicts with the program, one wouldn't think that I would be an asset for recruiting purposes. George, however, liked my hustle and the way I expressed myself. To him, I was an underutilized asset.

As much as I was learning and contributing, the directors of the program eventually decided that they wanted me to find a traditional assignment. I was technically hired into the rotational program and HR wasn't a track within that program. I was diligently searching for work, but I had less than six months' worth of experience.

With my newfound insight into the process, my interviewing skills were much improved, but I still lacked hard skill. A few of the interviews that I thought would be very promising, teams managed by my HBCU friends and mentors, also didn't yield results. "If only I had a little more experience…" they told me. And to be honest, I thought that was fair criticism even though we were friends.

Kizzy provided moments of fun and ease, but on balance, managing the relationship was slowly becoming a burden. She was out of her element. She'd been able to find work at an insurance company, but her insecurities were too close to the surface. No matter how much progress she made in life, she never accepted that she was no longer a girl from the trailer park.

In mid-November of 1999, I caught a break. Enron was in the process of developing a new online trading platform for various energy commodities and needed analysts to stress test the system and aid in development. While not an ideal assignment, this would solve my immediate problem of finding a legitimate position. The rotation program managers assured me the assignment wouldn't last more than 4 to 6 months, so I took it without hesitation.

Almost immediately, I saw that the assignment was oversold to me. The request for analysts was a generous exaggeration—what they needed were bodies to play with the interface and stress test for bugs and functionality. After the go live date, these people would be converted to help desk analyst to field trouble calls from users. Answering phones was not what I'd spent 5 years in school for. This was a dead-end job, and I wanted the quickest way out.

The ladies I worked with were the highlight of the opportunity. Most of them were in their thirties and forties with kids and families; their worries and concerns made my issues seem small and petty. The sacrifices of these working mothers put certain things into perspective for me.

Sadly, the women on the management team didn't appreciate the zeal I brought to work every day. They had a script they wanted to follow and didn't like me working faster than the pace they had set. I made a request for a transfer but was denied. They saw my efforts as an attempt to make them look bad rather than as a resource to be utilized. No one took more offense than Elaina.

Elaina was originally from Russia, but worked for Enron Europe in the London office. She was tall, beautiful, and intelligent with ambitions to match. Only in her late twenties, she was the chief consultant for the trading platform initiative. This was to be a stepping stone towards great things, and she wanted everything to conform to her plan.

Elaina had a fundamental issue with my participation within the group. Because I was able to rapidly assimilate the information presented and make an informed guess about the inner workings of the platform, I rarely asked for her help. As a result, the other members of the team began to seek my advice when they had questions. Whether her accent was too difficult for them to understand or her instructional methods unclear, I was an easier resource to leverage.

On one such occasion, Elaina began to chastise me for interfering with her lesson plan. She was the manager, she reminded me, and it wasn't my place to help anyone. I should know my place.

I could no longer listen to what she was saying, because I was more concerned with maintaining a professional demeanor. As she continued to chastise me, I was acutely aware of the implications of a black man losing composure in a corporate environment.

"Look at me when I'm talking to you!" she yelled while grabbing my arm.

"Don't touch me," I said with a cold fury.

As she released my arm and slowly backed away, the tense silence on the floor was interrupted by the arrival of the rest of the management team. I'm not sure if they were watching the scene as it unfolded, but they were keen to control the volatile situation.

"Rahmaan, can we speak to you in the conference room?"

"No. I need to get some air. I'll be back and we can talk then."

I took my walk to clear my mind and come up with a plan. I knew they would attempt to keep the situation quiet, so it was important I document what had occurred. Understanding that time was of the essence, I cut my walk short in order to write my statement for HR. Rebuffing their request to speak immediately, I began crafting my statement.

My arrest a few years prior was the perfect tutorial for understanding how to factually document a sequence of events; minimizing as much subjectivity and bias as possible. I was very conscious of the racial overtones of the situation, but I made a concerted effort to downplay them. It would have been easy to play on the racial fears of the corporate structure, but I refused to do that for a variety of reasons.

For one, I had no real proof. I'd been treated badly, but to say that these people had it out for me specifically because I was black would have been speculation. Maybe they just didn't like me. I could never assassinate someone's character in that manner without undeniable proof.

Additionally, it would have been the most obvious play. Even if I could have proven racist intent, what would be the ultimate outcome? Maybe I could have sued for the duration of my salary in the program, $100,000, but then what? My career would effectively be over. Things like this can't be hidden. Right or wrong, I would be branded a personality risk with few willing to bring me into their organization.

I've never wanted to be a victim. I didn't want favors, handouts, or shortcuts. I just wanted to work. I had a voice, talent, and ambition that I wanted to share with the world. I was out to win—not play for a participation ribbon. I only required a place where I could prove that I was as good as I thought I was.

In the meeting, I sat quietly as they struck a conciliatory tone full of apologies and a naked attempt to save face. They were suddenly very concerned with my desire to be on a team more aligned to my skill set and career ambitions. They would do me the favor of expediting my request as long as the incident with Elaina to be kept quiet.

"Thank you very much, but I think this would be best if we let HR figure it out. Here is a copy of my letter for your records; I have a copy and a copy has been forwarded to HR."

That was my last day on the team.

Year 23: Part 2 –
Standing On My Own

I found myself, once again, looking for a new assignment. The situation with Elaina was deemed a miscommunication—two talented individuals who found themselves in a teachable moment. The unspoken understanding was that I would be allowed one more chance to find a suitable assignment—the thirty-day window they extended was an overt reminder of my precarious status.

With the passing of each day, I felt the pressure mounting. I was in a literal race against the clock to save my job. I had no other option but to make this work. I called every contact I'd made during my time in Houston. I made it clear this was do or die for me and any opportunity or recommendation would be appreciated.

To my surprise, not one of my HBCU friends or mentors was of any help. They either couldn't or wouldn't refer any opportunities my way. This was stunning because a summer had been spent talking about family and looking out for one another. Now there was no support offered or received.

It was the kindness of strangers that provided me an opportunity to interview for the natural gas trading desk. The time I'd spent on recruiting trips and with a more diverse crowd was bearing fruit. No promises were expected or made, only a fair opportunity to present myself on my terms.

On the last day of my thirty-day extension, I waited for news, certain it was my last moments at Enron. Although I'd been able to complete several rounds of interviews for the natural gas trading group, I hadn't received an answer. With a 5 pm deadline, I was running out of time—and hope.

Kizzy kissed me goodbye knowing her man could come home unemployed. Despite our earlier issues, she had stuck with me—always a kind word of encouragement or a kiss to lift my spirits. Just as I made peace with the possible end of my career, the phone rang; gas trading had a position for me.

I walked into my late afternoon meeting with the analyst program HR team and was greeted with stiff smiles and nervous body language. They'd expected me to fail. I sat down and let the awkward silence linger a bit. This was a small victory and I was going to savor it.

"We hear you have some good news?"

"I do. I've been offered a position in gas trading."

"That's very good. We're so happy for you." Despite the kind words, their eyes betrayed their true feelings. They'd been ready to show me the door, but I ended up holding the winning hand.

"We were going to present you with separation papers today, but we don't need them now."

"Yeah....I guess not."

With work settled, I was able to put more focus on my

relationship with Kizzy. Our current apartment wasn't sufficient for our needs; the neighborhood not suitable for a young and sociable couple. After a brief search, Kizzy found a great little community in the Galleria district that provided the amenities we desired. Feeling positive about our future, we upgraded to a 2-bedroom townhome with a small patio.

Although my career had experienced a fair amount of volatility, she was slowly but steadily finding stability in her own. Aside from securing a position at an insurance firm, which was going well, she enrolled in classes at the local community college. I encouraged her to continue her education. I wanted her to imagine a future much brighter than her past and to pursue it aggressively.

The next few months were fun and relaxing—and a long time coming. Kizzy and I were finally able to experience the bliss of a happy and secure relationship. We spent much of our time exploring the city, dancing, and trying out cool new restaurants. Trips to the beach and one to Dallas to visit my uncle rounded out our adventures across Texas. The most enjoyable times we spent, however, were with each other at home. A few joints and a backyard barbeque pit were all the entertainment we needed.

Unfortunately, the tranquility would not last. Despite the gains I'd made at Enron, cracks were starting to form in the foundation I had built in my new position. My main responsibility was to consolidate the day's natural gas trades into one cohesive benchmark report. While this meant that I didn't have to report to work until around 3 pm, my nights regularly extended to the early morning hours. A normal week was no less than fifty hours—encompassing the time of day when your mind and body are naturally shutting down.

The report I was tasked with generating was fundamentally flawed, and I was having a difficult time keeping it functional. With only three days' worth of training, I was unprepared for the complexity of the report. It was comprised of over thirty independent trading books, assigned across five or six geographical regions—all aggregated into one master report. Encompassing all of Canada and the United States, this was the largest natural gas trading portfolio in the world. It was my responsibility to make sure all the numbers matched so that trades could be properly executed on the next trading day.

But no matter how many hours I worked or how hard I tried, the numbers were difficult to reconcile. As the days and weeks passed, I would find more and more mismatched numbers; the Texas desk, for example, would state that it had 1000 outstanding contracts, but my report would say it only had 990 contracts.

Sometimes a simple refresh could find the extra 10 contracts, but not always. To compound the problem, a refresh would frequently render another region's numbers incorrectly. After a few refreshes, if the number was still incorrect, I was supposed to manually type in an offsetting amount in a correction sheet. The most expensive game of whack-a-mole I'd ever played was solved by simply writing in any number that would make the game work.

Compounding the issue was my relationship with my director, Jeff. Any question asked of him was answered with exasperation—if it was acknowledged at all. Seeing his interactions with others on the desk, including other first year analysts, only illustrated that this was about me and not a general disposition.

He called one morning at 7 am—there was a problem with the numbers and I needed to come back to the office to explain what was wrong. Only three hours removed from a particularly brutal night, I had very few answers to offer.

For months, traders had been making trade strategies based on the numbers in my report but implementing against a different number in the system. They'd finally uncovered the discrepancy and looked to me for answers. Why hadn't I corrected this? Why didn't I let anyone know? Did I understand the implications of this?

I explained that I wasn't trained on it. I pushed all the buttons I was trained to push. I added all the numbers I was told to add. I didn't know anything more than what I had been told to do. My lack of answers only infuriated Jeff. The disgust on his face as he demeaned all of my efforts was apparent to the entire department as they tried not to listen to the yelling directed towards me.

The sense of failure weighed on my mind and spirit like a lead cloak. This would be the summary of my career: a street kid that talked himself into the halls of opportunity but was ultimately exposed. I had no business being there in the first place.

I needed air. My sense of failure grew as I made my way to my car. I sat with the engine running, fighting the urge to run, contemplating my many failures, and feeling the weight of my world pressing in on me. The more I thought about my failures, the worse I felt. The worse I felt, the more I thought about my failures. I was caught in a loop of despair that was slowly but surely crushing my spirit and will to continue.

I sat in my car and cried.

It was all too much to bear. I was hurt at the unfair manner in which I had been treated. I was disappointed in myself for not working harder and ashamed that I didn't know what the next step should be. I'd squandered all the good will that had brought me to this moment, letting untold numbers of people down. There was nothing else for me to do but cry.

And then I heard it. Through the fog of despair and the seeds of doubt that were taking root in my mind, a voice reached out and grabbed me by the heart. It was a song I'd heard many times but had failed to listen to: "The Line" by D'Angelo.

Each time the song ended, I played it again. And every time it played, a piece of me was restored.

I was done standing by, waiting for someone to tell me which way to go. I wasn't going to ask for permission or forgiveness. I was going to be me—for better or worse. If I was going to be fired, I was going out on my terms. I'd rather fail on my own than follow someone else off a cliff.

Year 23: Part 3 –
All Things Clearer in Time

As the days extended beyond my moment of self-awareness, I thought extensively on the issues facing me at work. The key issue wasn't the report, I realized. It had its share of shortcomings, but it wasn't the source of the problem. The issue was as basic as it was obvious: no one really understood how the system worked.

I assumed this was a system put in place by people much smarter than me. My managers had been there for years with decades more experience; how could they not know what was going on? The more excuses I made for them, the more obvious their shortcomings became. If I had any lingering doubts about this analysis, I only needed to refer back to the inadequate knowledge base they passed to me. I needed to find my own answers.

The first time I showed up to work at 8 am, I shocked a lot of people. Although my responsibilities didn't start until the late afternoon, my resources kept regular work hours. If I was going to leverage their knowledge, I needed to be available based on their schedule. We couldn't wait until the afternoon to test the systems; this is when they were required to be online. Any tests or changes had to occur earlier in the day.

The IT department would be the source of my answers. As much as Enron championed all things internet and IT, there was a glaring lack of interest as expressed by individual managers. IT was something that other people managed for them. Within gas trading, there was no interest for IT outside of system availability.

It was during my frequent visits to IT that I was introduced to Joseph. Joseph was a contractor working on an unrelated project, but increasingly found time to help me navigate some of my ideas and questions.

He was of South Indian decent and held deep Christian convictions; a combination I'd never encountered before or since. While we never discussed theology or politics in depth, I was impressed with the confidence his faith instilled in him. Not only was he deeply knowledgeable, but he went out of his way to share that knowledge and teach others. He was a mentor, and I greatly appreciated him.

For weeks, I put in 20-hour days. As they accumulated, I sensed a change in the way I was perceived. A few thought I was crazy: who would voluntarily subject themselves to such a strenuous schedule? But most of them showed an increased amount of respect and friendliness I hadn't experienced before.

They didn't understand what I was doing, but they knew I was dedicating myself to the task of improving the system and by extension their workloads. I was making allies.

It wasn't so off the mark to call it crazy although pathological would be a better description. As tired as I was, I was energized by the power I was accumulating. The more I learned, the more I wanted to learn. I took a perverse pleasure in pushing myself to my physical and mental limits in spite of all of my detractors. This was a test of wills and determination, and I refused to lose.

Every condescending look or comment that Jeff gave me only fueled my rage and pushed me harder. As I deconstructed each facet of the system, my mind was pushed to the limit trying to comprehend the full scope and enormity of the process. Despite the volume and weight of everything I was learning, I was finally having fun.

Eventually, I was able to determine the core problem: no one ever bothered to audit the reference tables in the database. When certain types of trades were issued, they couldn't be correctly attributed to the proper portfolio.

When I called the data in the evening, all trades without the proper tags would be excluded from my query. To complicate matters, the support desks used a separate system to account for trades; this is why their number would match their trader's number but wouldn't match mine.

I felt a strong sense of vindication. I'd taken months of abuse from management only to uncover a flaw in the system that preceded my tenure by an undetermined amount of time. More than proving anything to anyone else, I proved to myself that I was capable and competent. Through sheer determination and a stubborn will to succeed, I was able to experience my first taste of success. And I wanted more.

As sure as I was that I could improve on the reporting structure, I also knew I needed a vacation. All the 80-hour weeks had taken their toll and I needed to recharge. Naima's wedding was the perfect excuse to unwind. I hadn't seen my sister in a while, and with all the tables updated and the reports left in a fellow analyst's hands, I headed home to California.

Naima had joined the Army a few years prior and she seemed to be getting her life together. She'd always had a penchant for aligning herself with people of questionable ideals and character traits. Since joining the military, however, I'd noticed she was headed in a more positive direction.

Our family had reservations about her getting married at twenty years old, but we were happy and supportive of her and her new direction. My mother wanted this to be a special time for my sister and was going to do whatever she could to make it so. I found out that doing all she could meant bringing Dayna into the planning process.

I was surprised, though I shouldn't have been. My mother always loved Dayna. No matter my personal ups and downs with Dayna, she'd always been welcome in my home. She even had her own key to the family home. Despite not having spoken to her in years—and my being in a new relationship—she was part of the family, according to my mother. Even if I objected, my opinion would have little influence on the matter.

Too much time had passed for me to be concerned with any hurt feelings from years past. At that point in my life, my career was my chief concern—with little room for much else. Even though this singular focus was causing issues with Kizzy, I loved her and was content with my life.

Kizzy was also not happy that she couldn't join me. She'd been unable to get an entire week off from work, so we decided

I would go home alone to help with the wedding and she would fly out for the ceremony. Despite her disappointment, I knew we needed time away from each other. We were too quick to escalate a petty argument into something bigger than it deserved. Given the stress that I was under, I had little patience for her insecure moments. In my heart I knew she was having a hard time relating to me, but I needed her to take more responsibility for her own sense of security.

I made it a point to speak with Dayna as soon as I got to town. I wanted to air out any possible issues and either deal with them or table them for the sake of my sister's wedding. It wasn't long before we both realized that we had nothing but the best hopes and wishes for each other. Our separate lives had forced us to grow up and see the many errors of our ways. Despite being in new relationships, there was a genuine affection for each other, and we made a promise to always be friends.

This new and evolved dynamic was met with skepticism and outright challenges from our friends. They simply didn't believe that we were done with each other in a romantic way. As the week progressed and we met with more friends and family, this sentiment was echoed. It was hard for anyone to conceive of us as anything other than a couple. Our history was too deep and rich for anything else.

As good as the rapport was with Dayna, there was work to do. Key among my list of duties was making sure the groom felt welcome in the family. This task was harder than it seemed, because no one had met him before this.

Kevin and Naima met while she was stationed at Fort Hood in Texas. I don't recall ever hearing about him until the wedding announcement, but then again, my sister and I were never that close. I had a lot of reservations about her rush to marry, but I'd learned many years ago that she was going to do whatever she wanted; good advice be damned.

Two days before the wedding, my mother gave my sister a wedding shower at our house. My key contribution as the best man and brother of the bride would be to keep Kevin away for a few hours. He didn't seem to be in the mood for a party, and taking my sister's soon-to-be husband to a strip club didn't feel appropriate, so I got my friends together to have dinner and drinks with him in San Francisco.

Our first stop was Jabari's house to meet with everyone before heading out. As we waited for all the guys to arrive, Kevin seemed uncomfortable. He was getting along with everyone just fine, but he wasn't engaged in the conversation.

I figured he was just nervous, but there wasn't much I could do. He was getting married at twenty-one—nervous was part of the deal. Besides, I was on vacation and was intent on enjoying myself. The weed being passed around only added to the fun I was having.

It wasn't long before he asked to go back to my house.

"What's the matter?"

"I don't have any money. We forgot our bank cards in Texas."

"That's what's been bothering you?" I asked annoyed. "You don't need any money right now. I'm taking you out."

"But I want to pay for my own stuff!" he replied defiantly.

"Dude, I get it, but there's nothing you can do about it right now."

"I just need to talk to Naima. We have checks, but they're

out of state checks and no one will take them."

"Listen man, I get it but you're going to have to learn to accept help. If you're joining this family, you have to understand that we got you. I have money, so you have money. And my mother has money, so you're straight. We'll sort it out later."

I felt bad for the kid, because he didn't know me or the family he was entering. He was in an impossible situation and the idea of relying on strangers was difficult for him. I talked to him about the challenges that lay ahead. I told him about the pitfalls of unchecked pride and how asking for help was never a sign of weakness.

I tried to comfort him in the knowledge that we take family and loyalty seriously, and that he would be taken care of, *no matter what*. We could cash the checks on his behalf, or simply cover any costs and be paid back later.

He seemed to feel better about the situation, but he still wanted to go home to discuss the situation with my sister. At this point, I was willing to do whatever I could to solve this situation. He was being a drag, so I took him back home.

My hope was that it would only take a few minutes to set everything in order. Kevin found my sister and they went for a walk around the block to discuss their issues in private, and I tried my best to stay out of everyone's way.

As much as I wanted to keep to myself, there were a number of people that hadn't seen me in years and wanted to talk. My cousin Jamira, whom I hadn't seen in about five years, was the most surprised to see me. We'd never seen eye to eye, and she seemed to consider me to be an elitist, but she was still family.

I chatted with Dayna a little too, but I was getting tired of being in a house full of women. I had things I wanted to do, and my sister's problems were interfering with my plans. I could see them standing a few houses down the street still discussing things. Knowing that this problem wasn't going to resolve itself, I asked my mother to help them through it. Maybe another rational voice could move things along.

When the three of them returned to the house, I could tell a lot of tension had been released. The couple was happy to have their problems resolved and things were back to normal. Kevin, however, had had enough for the day and just wanted to relax at home. The women didn't seem to mind him hanging around, so I was more than happy to leave him there. Dayna and I made plans to see each other later that evening to finish a few more wedding details, but the next few hours were mine.

When I returned home a little while later, the peace I'd left had evaporated. Kevin and my sister were visibly upset, and my mother was angry. In the hours that had past, word had been relayed to my grandmother and father that Kevin was terrorizing the family.

From what my mother explained, Kevin supposedly stormed into the house during the party and verbally berated my sister in front of everyone. When my mother attempted to intervene, she was cursed out, and told to mind her own business. As a result of all of this, my father's family would not be attending the wedding.

I was stunned. I couldn't begin to fathom how this narrative had formed in the few hours I'd been gone. Anyone who knew my mother would know that disrespect wasn't something she accepted passively. Exasperated by the turn of events, my mother suggested I call my grandmother to sort everything out.

I was sure the whole situation was a misunderstanding that could be resolved with a short conversation. Any idea of a quick resolution, however, was dispelled as the phone call with my grandmother became more contentious.

Her mind was made up. She'd been told the entire story by my cousin Jamira, and that's all she needed to know.

"Granny, Jamira is a liar. She never heard the conversation between Kevin and Naima, because they never came in the house. She stayed in the house with me while they walked around the corner. I'm telling you, all that never happened. This is *me* telling you this."

"I don't know. I know what I've been told."

"Granny, please come to the wedding. Naima will be hurt if you don't come. I want to see you there."

I called my father to have a similar discussion with him. He'd heard the same story from his mother and was in a rage. Not only was he refusing to come to the wedding, he wanted to have a talk with Kevin, man to man. When he was done ranting, I relayed the same information I'd given his mother. He'd known my mother for nearly thirty years; had she ever been a person to accept disrespect from anyone without a fight?

I'm sure he flashed back to his many experiences with her, because he seemed to calm down a bit. It didn't make sense, he conceded, but he was still unhappy with the speed of everything. Acknowledging his concerns, I reminded him that the whole situation would be worse if he missed his daughter's wedding. More than ever, his presence was needed.

Securing his presence at the wedding, I ended the call and

talked to my mother about what had happened. I wasn't angry so much as I was feed up with my grandmother's act. The more I spoke to my mother, the more it became a vent for my lifelong issues with my grandmother.

For twenty-three years, she had treated my sisters and me with casual disdain. Sure, things were "okay" when we saw her or spoke to her, but the difference between her affections for us and my other cousins was palatable.

The missed birthdays, holidays, and special events of ours had accumulated over the years, but were forgiven out of duty to family. Always having to initiate contact on the holidays was bothersome, but we were taught to honor them, nonetheless. Making sure to go see her when I arrived in town from college was my way of giving her that honor, even though she never bothered to celebrate my academic accomplishments.

This event, however, was a step too far. To take all of that effort and forgiveness and throw it away to hurt my sister was too much. That fact that it was due to such an egregious lie was too much. As far as I was concerned, she was dead to me. If any of the other family members wanted to join, it was fine by me. I never liked them that much to begin with.

I was mentally exhausted. It wasn't exactly the vacation I'd hoped for, but I had responsibilities to tend to. Unexpectedly, Dayna had provided the few moments of peace and happiness I experienced. The fights and misunderstandings of the past were hard to recall—those that were seemed quaint and insignificant in light of the people we'd become. Our significant others were lucky to have the updated versions of us, we laughed.

I was happy to have Dayna come by later that evening. There

were minor details that needed our attention; we also wanted to spend a few hours relaxing before things got really hectic. My mother's family was due to arrive the next day, but more importantly, Kizzy would be arriving as well.

Dayna and I talked and laughed about anything and nothing as the evening progressed into the night. She was confused and pissed off about the events of the afternoon, but she'd known my thoughts and feelings concerning my father's family for years.

She shared her apprehensions about the upcoming school year and her pending exchange year in Spain (she'd taken my advice, even though she hated me at the time). I told her about the pressures of Enron, the project I'd been working on, and my plans to expand its scope. And we talked about our relationships—the good parts, the shortcomings of our mates, and a desire to just be happy.

After we finished planning for the wedding, she suggested watching a movie at home; the idea of going out was too much to contemplate given our current levels of exhaustion. Turning the television on in my room, we laid on the bed to finish our conversation. There wasn't much on at midnight, but we were happy for the added distraction.

As we fell silent watching the flickering images, I began to notice a change in the atmosphere. It was difficult to describe at first, but the air began to feel denser. The room became warmer even though the temperature had not changed. I was very aware that Dayna was lying next to me.

As she leaned into me and placed her head on my shoulder, we stared at the television in silence. Aside from the arm I placed around her shoulder, I was afraid to move or say a word. This was right, although so very wrong. I smelled her hair (that familiar smell I'd known so intimately over the years), and knew that she and I could never be just friends. I was in love with her, just as I'd been since the moment I'd laid my eyes on her at homecoming all those years ago.

She must've been reading my thoughts, because her body seemed to match mine in the way it laid there fighting what it wanted. We both had people we loved, and to do what we wanted would have been a violation of the trust they'd bestowed upon us.

"You should go home," I said, slowly getting up and walking out the room.

"I know."

Year 23: Part 4 – True Colors

Despite the drama preceding the marriage ceremony, the entire event was one of celebration and joy. Dayna, however, was visibly shaken and unhappy—at least to me. Tension had given way to an uneasiness that was difficult for us to shake.

The pain and disappointment in my choices since our last split was too much for Dayna to bear. Celebrating a wedding with my mother's extended family that didn't include taking my last name was a reality that she'd never imagined.

To make matters worse, Kizzy was an embarrassment to me. In the harsh light of my family, this fact became clear. Kizzy's stripper-influenced style of dancing at the reception only confirmed my family's poor opinion of her. Being gracious, they treated her with kindness and respect, but I knew they weren't thrilled in my choice of mate.

Dayna's presence only made the differences between the two more stark. My family clearly had a preference—though they went to great lengths to respect the relationship boundaries that Dayna and I had erected. Still, they were equally unimpressed with her boyfriend when they met him at the wedding ceremony. In my heart, I knew that my remaining days with Kizzy would be few.

While the remainder of our time in California was uneventful, our return to Houston also marked a return to the same old arguments that had been plaguing us. Our relationship could no longer thrive.

Living in our townhouse was a problem for her. According to her, we were living too well, and she was losing her edge. She was finding it hard to concentrate on her education and career, because she was betraying who she *really* was. In her mind, the solution was to move out for thirty days and make things difficult for herself in order to recapture her fighting spirit. It was the dumbest thing I'd ever heard.

Unlike her, I remembered clearly where I'd come from. More importantly, I vividly recalled all the effort to leave it behind. I didn't miss the government cheese and syrup sandwiches of my youth. I didn't rhapsodize the violence in the neighborhood or the lack of resources. I hated the feelings of vulnerability and lack of power that living in poverty instilled.

The $40k I was making each year still didn't make me feel like I'd moved far enough from that past. I was never going back. And if that's what she needed, she was clearly not the woman for me. If she moved out, we would have to start from the beginning.

Aside from a few disagreements about what she could take with her (she had a particular affinity for a computer desk I'd purchased for her birthday but for my computer), it was a relatively painless breakup. There was a need to simplify my home life; my attention was needed elsewhere.

In my absence, all the work I'd done to correct the systematic issues plaguing our reporting system had begun to pay dividends. There was a period of testing conducted by my peers, Robin and

Gabriel, while I was gone, but the official rollout was finalized shortly after my return. When Jeff addressed the team to highlight the changes made and our new level of veracity, I experienced a growing sense of pride for what I had been able to accomplish. It wasn't until he attributed full credit for our system upgrades to Robin and Gabriel that my pride evaporated— replaced with cold, raging hatred.

I could tell they were extremely uncomfortable with the sequence of events. They knew the effort they contributed was minimal, and it bothered them to have so much praise heaped upon them without merit. Still, their sense of shame wasn't enough to compel them to speak up.

"Why didn't you guys say anything?" I asked when we had a moment to ourselves.

"I don't know. I didn't know what to do or say about that," Robin said.

"Hey man, we're sorry," Gabriel added.

And that was all that was offered. As angry and as hurt as I was, there was nothing I could do about it. I still knew something no one else did: the changes I'd implemented were only the opening act to a much grander plan.

With a renewed sense of motivation, I set about the task of revolutionizing the entire system. This time, however, my efforts were far subtler. I no longer sought the advice or input from many of my peers due to all the information I'd previously gathered, but mostly because I didn't trust anyone.

The reception of the new system was more than I could have hoped for. I can't fully explain the feeling of validation and pride I experienced as each person congratulated me on the good work.

Even Jeff's half-hearted compliment couldn't dampen what I'd been able to achieve: at twenty-three, I was able to redesign the largest trading report for natural gas in the world, ensuring 100% accuracy and saving the company hundreds of man hours a month. Most importantly, I proved to myself that I belonged.

Having finally achieved a sense of security and accomplishment with my career, I was able to devote my attention to my continuing problems with Kizzy. Although she had moved out, we were never out of contact, as there was a sense that we could work things out.

Despite our disagreements, she was still my friend. When she asked if she could use my car one Saturday to go to work, I didn't think much of it. Always an advocate for making money, I was more than willing to help.

Around 11 a.m., I called to make sure she was able to meet the schedule we'd set. She was in a good mood; work was progressing well and she would be done shortly. She asked if I would like to eat with her; there were some things she wanted to discuss. Never being comfortable going into meetings without knowing the agenda, I wanted an idea of what she had in mind. In the sweetest voice possible, she asked for the computer desk.

This was an old argument that I thought was dead.

While I appreciated the nature and protocol of gift-giving, I had a fundamental issue with her request. She had no real use for the desk. It was designed for use with a computer—which she didn't have. She was also moving into her friend's apartment on a temporary basis, which had no room for a large piece of furniture. Above all, we both assumed that she would be moving back in at some point.

My insistence that the desk remain with me didn't sit well with her. The sweetness from her initial request was replaced with anger and defensiveness. As her anger grew, her complaints expanded beyond the computer desk to encompass every perceived slight or wrong she'd endured from me.

The irony of her borrowing my car that very morning, while berating me on how I never supported her, was missed. To me, she was being ungrateful, and I was tired of her antics. I told her bring my car to me immediately, and I hung up the phone.

I tried to remain calm as time ticked by. Houston had notoriously bad traffic, especially in the Galleria area. When my phone rang and my caller ID identified her, I was slightly annoyed. As she tried to plead her case for the desk one more time, I quickly cut her off.

"You don't even have a computer. What you need to worry about is getting my car back to me—like now!"

When another twenty minutes passed and she hadn't returned, I called her to press the issue. The phone rang unanswered. The rush of anger and anxiety threatened to overtake me, but I suddenly felt a wave of calm wash over me. She wanted me to be angry and feel bad. She *wanted* to make me feel the sense of loss she must have been feeling.

I had to call Reggie to pick me up for our trip to the mall. He was far more bothered about the situation than I was. I could understand his perspective, but I had to maintain a certain amount of emotional distance from it. The only purpose anger would serve would be to fuel more anger.

Returning from the mall, I found that Kizzy hadn't returned. I tried to call her a few times, but there was still no answer. She was probably out with her friends, laughing at me. I knew she'd have her fun and eventually return in the morning, expecting me to give in to her.

But morning came, and she still wasn't back. I had to give her credit for holding out as long as she had, but it was time to put this nonsense behind us. I ended up taking a bus to work, and Reggie gave me a ride home. As I filled him in on everything, my phone rang.

"Hello?"

"Hi…"

"Where are you?"

"What?" I was sure she'd heard me.

"Where are you?" I asked again, getting frustrated.

"I'm at the casino…"

"CASINO?!" But she didn't reply.

The call had dropped. I tried to call her back, but there was difficulty making a connection. By this time, I was angry. The nearest casino was in Lafayette—a few hours away.

"What she say?" Reggie asked

"She's at the casino," I replied

"Casino? What Casino?"

As I started to say Louisiana, I paused. Something didn't feel right. Why would she go to Louisiana? She wasn't a gambler. Then it hit me. *She was in Vegas.*

The phone rang.

"Where are you?" I asked, even though I knew the answer.

"I'm on the strip."

"Las Vegas?"

"Yeah…"

As I explained the situation to her, I made sure to convey the living hell my mother would rain on her if she wrecked that car (it was still in her name at the time). The last thing either of us needed was for my mother to have a vested interest to interject herself into this mess.

Reg was livid. He couldn't believe the audacity of her to take advantage of the situation the way she had. The more we talked, the more he was bothered by my lack of response. Crazy wasn't something that needed to be understood, but recognized and respected. I respected her crazy, and I needed to remain calm and focused in order to get away unscathed.

When she finally arrived, gone were the fire and anger, replaced with fear and pain. I had no words for her, only an embrace and the feeling of a love lost.

Over the next few weeks, we were friendly but I kept my distance. Still, I cared for her, so I'd check in on her periodically to see how her schooling was progressing. It was during one such conversation, that I learned the full extent of the trouble that she was in.

For all intents and purposes, she was homeless. She'd had a major fight with her friend and was asked to leave. It escaped her that she couldn't wear her friend's clothes without permission. She'd been forced to accept a space with another friend, but it was less than ideal. Her new living arraignment consisted of a pallet in the same room he pressed homemade bullets.

His girlfriend wasn't pleased with the arrangement either. Feeling partially responsible for her being in Houston, I offered my couch to her with the understanding that we would not be getting back together and that she should be working to secure more permanent accommodations.

It was only a few, short weeks before things went south. Before Kizzy moved back in, I'd visited Naima and Kevin at Fort Hood a few hours from Houston. While there, I'd met someone at a local club and she was close to being discharged from the Army. We spent the weekend with each other and made tentative plans to see each other again a few weeks later.

Her plan was to drive from Texas to her home in Florida. I had no illusions that we would be a long-term couple, but it would be nice to spend a weekend together.

A few days before she was to arrive, I informed Kizzy that I would be having company (I was light on detail) and that she should make arrangements for the weekend. She accepted the news with cheerful acknowledgement.

When I got home from work that Friday, I found Kizzy still there. I was extremely annoyed, but calmly asked her when she would be leaving. Before we could sort the details, my guest arrived.

I knew Kizzy was sometimes attracted to women and was curious about my guest—who was also attracted to women. But I wasn't keen on opening that door with Kizzy. Luckily, Kizzy left while Army Girl and I showered, changed, and left for an evening out.

After a drama-free night of dinner, cocktails, and smoky jazz, we headed back to my place. When we arrived, I found Kizzy in my bedroom and spare linens on the couch. Asking Army Girl to give me a minute, I walked to the bedroom to handle the situation.

"What are you doing?"

"I'm doing homework…"

"I can see that, but what are you doing in my room?"

"I decided to stay."

"Okay, whatever. Can you do your homework in the living room? We're going to listen to some music in here."

"Where are you going to sleep?"

"Where I always sleep—in my bed."

"And where is she sleeping?"

"With me," I said authoritatively.

"Fuck that!"

I was learning first-hand the maxim that no good deed goes unpunished.

"Um…you'll be sleeping on the couch tonight," Kizzy informed Army Girl and walked back into my bedroom.

Now I was angry.

"You have no right to say who's sleeping where. This is my house and everyone else is a guest. You know what? You are no longer welcome here. I need you to leave."

I can't remember what was said, but we were yelling over each other as she retreated farther into my room. As I followed her, she climbed on top of the bed as if to claim it as her territory. With my anger rising, I reached up to pull her down from the bed, but she began to flail her arms and resist, culminating with a punch to my chest.

Enraged, I pushed her down on the bed and as she kicked at me wildly, I attempted to grab one of her legs. I used all of my strength to pull. I pulled too hard, and tossed her across the room. Landing with a thud, Kizzy moaned loudly before passing out.

I was in trouble. I was a black man with an unconscious woman on his bedroom floor and another girl sitting on his couch—in Texas. I let that idea sit for a bit. It was going to be difficult to explain, but I'd watched enough television to know that the cover-up is always worse than the original crime.

I dialed 911 and explained the situation to dispatch. As I awaited my fate, Army Girl stared at me. I was surprised she hadn't left, but I was glad for the company.

As I spoke to the two white male police officers who arrived, the retelling made it clear how big a fool I actually was. The police officers seemed to agree, because they just stared at me when I finished explaining.

"Whose apartment is this?" one of them asked.

"It's mine."

"And her name isn't on the lease?"

"No sir."

And with that, it was over. They radioed dispatch, explained what they'd found, and informed them to contact the nearest hospital to prepare for a new patient. As they left and carried her out, one of the officers paused and said over his shoulder:

"Pick your girls better, young man, and make better decisions."

Year 24: Part 1 – I Think It's Better That I Tell You Now

"Oh babe!" Dayna sighed.

She was amused but disappointed as I recounted the conclusion of Kizzy and me. By now Dayna was in Spain, but thanks to Enron's international presence and telecom plan, we were able to resume our late-night calls. It might have been a bit unethical, but fuck them; it was no more unethical than anything I'd been asked to do.

The time we shared during the wedding had changed us. At the moments in our lives when we were fighting against the currents, trying to stifle our ambitions, we were reintroduced to the essence of who we were—and always had been—to each other.

The future was heavy on our minds. I was completing my year's assignment in gas trading, while she was a semester away from completing her year abroad. The more we danced around the idea of a future together, the stronger and clearer that reality became. We needed to be together, if only to protect others from us, we laughed. In December, I told her I loved her.

Our future would not include Texas. Her desire to live anywhere but Houston was only matched by my desire to put Enron behind me. Despite being one of the fastest-growing companies in the country, its corrosive environment would only serve to facilitate the worse aspects of my personality.

Greed and callousness weren't ideals I aspired to—I wanted something greater. The mediocre review I received despite the innovation I'd wrought only underscored my desire to leave. I didn't need their approval; my work spoke for itself. The only thing I needed from Enron was a high stock price when I cashed in my options once I resigned.

As luck would have it, I secured a position with Pacific Bell in San Francisco—flush with a five-figure payout from my Enron options—I decided to spend a month in Spain with Dayna. International travel had always been a life goal I'd hope to experience, but I didn't think it would happen until well after my mid-twenties.

With a care package of American foods and makeup for one of Dayna's friends, I boarded my first international flight to Madrid. I thought about the young black boy I'd been, dreaming of a better life as he walked through the ghettos of East Oakland.

The hopes, dreams, and anger experienced over the previous two decades had forged a man capable of fulfilling the promises made by that child. I accepted that moment for all it represented: the payment of a life debt and a deposit on an inspiring life with the woman I loved.

Finally.

My arrival to the Iberian Peninsula was an assault of the senses. Decades of heavy tobacco use lent a thickness to the air of the airport terminal. Beneath a *PROHIBITO FUMAR* sign, a woman was smoking, adding a touch of irony to the scene. Unfortunately for me, that was the extent of my high school Spanish. Exhausted from the long flight—with a distinct language barrier and Dayna nowhere to be found—I was overwhelmed.

I navigated the corridors of the airport, mostly by following other passengers, and found my way to baggage claim. At customs, I received the first stamp in my passport. The sound the stamping machine made sent a warm wave through my body. It was official: I was a world traveler. The only thing left to do was find my way out of the maze and into the arms of my love.

She was wearing a green plaid skirt with a lavender blouse, hair and makeup styled as if she had somewhere important to be. As I took her into my arms, her familiar scent the only thing between us, I had one thought: *this is the beginning of the rest of my life*.

The apartment she shared in the Los Carmenes district was the family home of her roommate. It was a place that had witnessed countless birthdays, family dinners, and holidays. I immediately felt at ease.

I was tired and needed to clean up after such a long flight, so I opted to take a shower while Dayna completed errands in the neighborhood. As I washed the grime of travel from me, I reflected on the changes I'd noticed in the girl I loved.

She seemed more mature than the last time I'd seen her. There was a quiet confidence and strength that, while not new, was more pronounced. She was growing into the strong, sexy, classy woman I always knew her to be. I knew how lucky I was to have another chance to do right by her.

When I heard someone enter the apartment, I stepped out of the bedroom and came face to face with Dayna's roommate. I introduced myself and extended my hand in greeting, but she grabbed me in a firm hug and kissed me on both cheeks. In shock, I pulled away.

We'd spoken only a couple of times when I'd called Dayna, but I didn't think our relationship had reached a physically affectionate level. More importantly, I was concerned about what Dayna would think if she saw her roommate kissing on me.

When Dayna returned, I pulled her to the side to explain what happened. I didn't feel guilty, but I was uncomfortable with the breach of protocol. As she exploded in laughter, I was even more confused and embarrassed. When she finally caught her breath, she explained that physical affection was the Spanish way.

More specifically, greeting personal acquaintances and friends with a hug and a kiss on both cheeks was the social norm. It was, in fact, very rude to refuse such things—akin to not shaking a hand extended in greeting.

Welcome to Spain.

Later, we listened to the new Jill Scott CD I promised she'd love and talked about nothing in particular, content in the knowledge that we had the rest of our lives for deeper conversations. Before long, the day caught up to me and I went to sleep.

A few hours later, I woke feeling refreshed and eager to see more of Madrid. With a trip to the Canary Islands planned the next morning, I wanted to get a basic feel for the city I would call home for the next month. Dayna didn't match my sense of urgency. People didn't go out until late, she explained. It was normal to have dinner closer to midnight rather than the early evening meals we were used to.

Just past midnight, we caught a cab and made our way to Sol, the center of Madrid and the figurative center of Spain. The sights and sounds of this historic center were beyond anything I'd ever seen. Although it was only Thursday, there was a festive mood in the atmosphere. Everyone seemed upbeat and fresh—a feeling closer to happy hour than closing time. We ate a brief dinner and made our way to a club where one of her friends tended bar.

As it turns out, this friend was the reason I'd brought a package of makeup all the way from the United States. My excitement was growing. This was a place for beautiful people, I noticed. Everyone was stylishly dressed and dancing to the familiar sounds of hip-hop and Top 40 pop songs.

It was as if the club was welcoming me with an ode to my culture and heritage. As I caught the eye of a raven-haired beauty, she smiled with a gleam in her eye like I was a gift at Christmas. *Oh yeah, this was going to be fun!* I just needed to remember to keep my eyes on my own paper.

Stepping up to the bar, Dayna greeted her friend warmly and introduced me as I handed her the makeup. With affection and gratitude, she hugged me tightly and raved about how I was a lifesaver. She was also from the U.S., and said it was difficult to consistently find makeup in Spain that accented her brown skin properly. She showed her gratitude with the extension of an open bar.

And that is when the evening took a right and a left turn at the same time. The Cape Cods that I requested (don't judge, I was only twenty-four) were heavy on Belvedere and extremely light on cranberry juice. Some might have described it as a splash of juice. Either way, the combination of travel, little rest, and strong drink created a sense of euphoria which I embraced with a firm grip.

Dayna and I danced the night away, intermixed with numerous drinks from her bartender friend. I lost count at number four. This must have been what heaven was like. The throbbing bass, beautiful women, exotic locale, along with being in love, created a nirvana that I never wanted to end.

We finally left the club around 4 a.m. Our flight to the Canary Islands was at 10 a.m. and I was eager to get home to get a few hours' sleep. The movement of the car was almost too much to bear. When we finally arrived at the apartment, I quickly stripped down and climbed into bed to sleep off my intoxication.

The alarm belligerently brought me out of a drunken coma into a world of nausea, bright lights, and loud noises. I'd had maybe an hour and a half of sleep, and it only seemed to make the situation worse.

The cab ride on the way to collect the friends that were accompanying us was more like that of a carnival. Each sharp turn, rapid acceleration, and deceleration was getting to be too much. Rolling down the window provided a brief respite from my agony. As the car waited for a red light to change, I took the opportunity to repaint the side of the white taxi.

The rest of the morning was a haze. We eventually picked up

our companions and arrived at the airport shortly after, where I found a seat to pass out. We had spent far too much time waiting on her friends to come out of their apartment, causing us to miss our flight. To make matters worse, the trip had been booked via a travel agency and the airline agent had no power to rebook us. The only course of action would be to revisit the original travel agency—on the other side of town—and have them rebook the trip.

My personal compulsion for punctuality was muted by my desire to pass out again. The idea of traversing across town in another cab was almost too much to comprehend. By default, I came up with a perfect plan: Dayna and her friends could journey across town and I could stay in the airport, pass out, and mind our bags.

She agreed, and I could sense her growing frustration. As she tied a luggage strap to my arm, I started to pass out. I understood how drunken bums could manage to sleep anywhere.

Year 24: Part 2 – A New Way to See Things

When we arrived in the Canary Islands a few hours later, I was thoroughly wrung out. Too much travel and alcohol—and not enough rest—had taken its toll. I knew I was letting Dayna down. I was embarrassing her in front of her friends and casting doubt on all the wonderful things she'd told them of me. In all honesty, I was letting myself down because I wanted to be better for her, but her growing attitude was akin to kicking me when I was down.

Waking up to the Gatorade I'd requested and no girlfriend in sight, I tried to get myself together. Hurriedly, I drank one bottle and started sipping on the next as I made my way to the second suite we'd rented. I found her chatting, laughing, and cutting onions for the dinner being prepared. Suppressing the urge to gag from the onions, I leaned in to kiss her check. She obliged but was cold in her acceptance. I was firmly in the dog house.

"Why are you so irritated with me?" I asked when I was able to get her alone. "You've been mad at me all day. What did I do?"

"You've been avoiding everyone all day. I've told all my friends how great you were, but you've been irritable all day."

"I've been sick all day!" I protested.

"No one told you to get so damned drunk." she retorted.

"It's not like I meant to get sick!" I pleaded.

It wasn't the easiest conversation and it required a number of apologies from me, but in the end we worked everything out. I was also feeling much better at that point. Hydration, rest, and youth had performed their magic.

As the evening progressed and we joined the Carnival festivities, Dayna loosened up noticeably—to the point where she started to poke fun at me. There was no malice intended, but it was getting under my skin. It didn't help that I was surrounded by people I didn't know.

At the Carnival, I was the only one not drinking—and since I knew how to drive a standard transmission—I became the designated driver. Driving around a bunch of loud, obnoxious, drunk people, coupled with Dayna's incessant sarcasm, was pushing me into a bad place.

I let her and her friends make their way into the mob of cross-dressed men and scantily costumed women dancing to the throbbing music while I sought out relatively less chaotic areas along the fringes of the crowd. I didn't want to be there.

Aside from the first few hours of our reunion, this entire trip had been an exercise in patience—of which I had little to give. The old frictions and mismatched ways of being were starting to resurface. I knew the high school sweetheart angle wasn't going to be enough to sustain us, and I didn't feel like trying to find a better one. As the evening progressed, I had the sinking feeling that I'd made a huge mistake coming to Spain. The knot of anger in my chest burned with acidic fury.

Walking through the venue lost in my own thoughts, I stumbled into Dayna and her friends. She danced around me, her starry-eyed gaze fixated on my angry one, smiling her seductive smile. The test of wills—hers of love and mine of fear and anger—was all that was present in that moment. As she touched me, my pride and ego gave way. She took my fear, anger, and pain in hand and cast it aside like dust in the wind.

When we finally returned to Madrid, we were able to reconnect in a more genuine way. During the day, she attended her classes at the university, and I wandered around the city trying to understand the place that had reshaped the woman I loved.

Our afternoons and evenings were spent together, sharing meals or exploring landmarks and recounting places I'd discovered. We quickly settled into a routine and began to rediscover the foundation of friendship we'd always known.

My own growth in Madrid was the catalyst to truly understanding what I'd sensed in Dayna from the moment I arrived. Those first few days were an exercise in managing frustration, with patience not being a virtue I was naturally blessed with.

For instance, Dayna had instructed me to purchase a monthly pass for public transit, but I didn't understand how to make the purchase. One would think you could purchase a pass at the local metro station, but the agent only stared blankly at me as I tried in English to explain what I wanted. It was later that I learned I had to go to a tobacco shop to purchase a pass.

Conducting business or banking was another issue. Famous for its siestas and long lunches, the whole of Madrid seemed to shut down around the same time I would make it to the center of town. Although most businesses would reopen, banks didn't seem to be on the same schedule as everyone else. Given that the advent of widespread credit/debit card use hadn't made it to Europe at the time, there were several days I would return home in disgust, comforted only by my sense of American superiority.

Soon after, we departed Madrid for our next excursion. Her exchange group was conducting a cultural exploration trip of Western Spain and we were looking forward to joining them. Although it was only a two-day trip, the itinerary was compelling. Our first destination would be the city of Merida to see ancient Roman ruins, followed by time in the city of Caceres.

In Merida, we visited the local museum renowned for its collection of Roman artifacts. Any well-regarded historical museum contains Roman artifacts, but this one was special because they were locally sourced: the town was founded by Romans in the first century. Walking through the museum, designed with arches reminiscent of classic Roman architecture, we felt as if we were momentarily transported to a time long gone. The love and pride of the museum personnel was evident, and we felt blessed to have shared their hospitality.

As wonderful as the museum was, two of the ancient jewels of Merida were only a short walk away: the local coliseum and Roman theater. To walk on the floor of an actual coliseum generated a cascade of conflicting thoughts. On one hand, it was cool to share space with such an iconic piece of history, although only a mini version of its much more famous cousin in Rome.

On the other, imagining the thousands of people and animals that surely died on that spot for sport was a strange notion to comprehend. My excitement for being there, mixed with a macabre titillation of the history of the place, left me solemn and contemplative.

The Roman theater was equally impressive, but for different reasons. I'd read many of the great Greek tragedies—imagining them performed live and for the first time in the days of antiquity left me envious. The ornate columns, busts, and stadium seating created and intimate atmosphere, the feelings of stagecraft and magic clinging to the air…

When our day in Merida was complete, we made the hour trip to Caceres for the remainder of the evening. After checking into our lodgings, Dayna and I—with a few of her friends—wandered around town looking for a restaurant. We couldn't agree on anything until someone spotted a Chinese restaurant on the second floor of a building.

We all shared a high level of curiosity about what we would find once inside. From an American perspective, we are fairly cognizant of immigrant groups coming to our country, but there tends to be a blind spot when it comes to other countries.

The ambiance was fairly typical of any basic Chinese restaurant, and we laughed at our naivety; what else did we expect? The one detail that was endlessly hilarious was that the staff spoke Spanish with strong Chinese accents. As we ate dinner and consumed several beverages, we laughed knowing that we were the joke, our naïve and limited perspectives being the punchline.

Continuing our journey through the city, we made our way

to the Plaza Mayor. With no real agenda, Dayna and her girlfriends decided to walk some more while her guy friend and I went to buy beer and relax in the square.

Finishing our 40 ounce beers, we began to notice a change in our surroundings. The once sparsely occupied square was quickly filling with young people. As the population of youth increased, the mood in the air changed from quiet to raucously festive. Before long, I found myself in a full-blown street party. In some areas, people played radios, and in others guitars and bongos were produced with jam sessions in full swing. The alcohol and marijuana were ubiquitous and freely passed.

It was an amazing scene of revelry and mirth, and the feeling was contagious. After walking around for a while and taking in the sites, we came across a friendly group near the steps leading to the hilltop cathedral. The guy I was with started a conversation with a few of the girls and I did my best to keep up with my limited Spanish. When I was asked a question, I responded the best I could, which elicited laughter and a flurry of comments from the girls—in Spanish.

Sensing that there was no malice intended yet still curious, I asked for a translation. I was a very handsome man, yet I spoke like a baby, one of the girls said. Apparently, the juxtaposition was endearing and sexy. I was flattered, drunk, and slightly embarrassed. I changed the subject to quiet the drunk, mischievous thoughts I was having, and asked why everyone was in the square.

"Asi…es Sabado," the cute girl replied.

It's Saturday. The weight of those words pressed into my ears and wormed their way through my drunkenness.

"For as long as anyone can remember," she continued, "everyone meets in the square just to hang out."

For weeks I'd walked past monuments, castles, and plazas rich with history. They were obviously grand and historic, but being in that square on that night meant so much more. It felt like a religious rite of passage to share that moment with complete strangers, sipping their liquor and smoking their weed. Because communing with humanity was what one did on Saturday in an ancient square built specifically for that purpose.

Once we were back in Madrid, we settled into our "old" routine. Dayna had lessons in the morning hours, and I slept far too late, frantically trying to get to Sol or some other commercial district before siesta.

I'm not sure why, but doors began to fascinate me. Maybe it was the many ornate designs I would encounter. Perhaps it was the hundreds of years of history I imagine had occurred behind them. I spent many hours contemplating this newfound appreciation.

Late afternoon would find me closer to home. Knowing she had a long day, I wanted to have dinner ready for her. A wonderful perk of the neighborhood is that one could buy any food item in its freshest state. The produce shops were splashes of bright color, while the cheese mongers were liberal with their pungent and savory samples. My favorite, however, was the poultry butcher that resided on the ground floor of our building.

The little old lady knew no English, but she was patient enough with my Spanish that we soon worked out a system. She took pride in slicing fresh chicken breast for me daily, punctuated with a smile and a nod. I frequently had to tend to a few stray feather shafts that were missed in the plucking process, but they were a testament to the freshness of the meat. A brief stop into the bakery next door for a baguette, and I had all I needed to prepare a meal for my lady.

As we approached St. Patrick's Day—my third weekend in Spain—we decided to visit Barcelona and Valencia with the same group of friends we'd traveled to the Canary Islands with. None of us had visited Barcelona before and there was something called Las Falles in Valencia that looked appealing. Because we had more free time, Dayna and I were tasked with securing our transportation between the cities.

Although we were spending a lot of time with each other, this particular day seemed special. As we approached and entered a beautiful building I'd seen a number of times during my walks, I was shocked and excited to find out that it was only a train station. The Atocha station, in its wrought iron style, seemed too grand for something as mundane as a train station.

After securing train tickets to Barcelona and renting a car from Barcelona to Madrid (via a day trip to Valencia), Dayna and I sipped espresso and ate pastries. The green canopy of trees bathed us in a soft light; birds darted between them as we watched turtles play in the pond.

If Madrid was a stylish and sophisticated woman, then Barcelona was her down-to-earth and more popular sister. Both cities were beautiful and intriguing, but Barcelona gave you the impression that the next great party was around the corner. From its rolling hills to its glittering shore and warm costal breeze, Barcelona smiled and embraced us.

The architectural masterpieces of Gaudi are some of the most prominent and well-visited landmarks in Barcelona. As few things do, each one lived up to their reputation as a must-see tourist attraction. Casa Mila and Parque Guell were impressive for their whimsical interpretations of the common apartment building and city park. The latter property was especially breathtaking due to its expansive views of the city and coast. It was La Sagrada Familia, however, that provided the most soul-moving experience.

The evening before our visit to La Sagrada Familia, we spent most of our time in the Gothic Quarter. The warren of streets and passages were a life size maze concealing many treasures; their revelation providing thrills of excitement. The mellow high of hash cigarettes enhanced the feelings of euphoric discovery and playfulness as we wandered aimlessly through the labyrinth. As we stumbled around a corner and into an expansive square, our mood quickly changed.

Before us stood one of the most awe-inspiring churches any of us had seen. The Catedral de Barcelona, with its gargoyles and towers, was a true work of art. Illuminated by the many spotlights arranged around its façade, it glowed powerfully in the evening darkness. The full weight and power of the Holy Church were imbued into its configuration.

The longer I stood in its shadow, the more uncomfortable I felt. The lines and angles were a little too sharp, almost menacing in their design. I could imagine how an uneducated peasant farmer would be intimidated and easily controlled by this display of power and might. The more I let my thoughts wander, the more I didn't like that church. Or maybe I was feeling a growing dislike for *The Church*—it was hard to sort it all out through my hash high.

I was expecting a similar feeling as we walked down the avenues towards La Sagrada Familia. The church looked like something from a nightmare. Knowing that Gaudi had become consumed with its construction, neglecting all other tasks—including his health until his untimely death—only added to the air of foreboding that I felt.

Although both La Sagrada Familia and Catedral de Barcelona were imposing in size, the energy of this church was vastly different than the gothic cathedral. Whereas the Catedral de Barcelona seemed to embody the rigidity of the Holy Church, the La Sagrada Familia embodied the free-flowing ease of the natural world.

The carvings of birds, frogs, fish, and other wildlife added to the theme of nature, life, and harmony. It was only then that I understood the passion of the man that had conceived so many masterful works of art. He loved the world and its natural beauty created by a loving God, and quested to find the many answers to life hidden in its mystery.

Year 24: Part 3 – All Good Things…

We left Barcelona for Valencia early Monday morning in a 4-cylinder hatchback. With no cruise control, I was forced to be more mindful of my speed. It didn't take me long to discover that five adults in such an underpowered car was its own form of speed control. I literally had to put the pedal to the metal in order to maintain a cruising speed of around 75 mph.

We arrived in Valencia in the early afternoon and headed to the beach to relax before the evening festivities began. There were a lot of people in town, but it was eerily tranquil in many places. As the crew settled on the beach, Dayna and I decided to take a walk along the water line.

I held her hand firmly as we walked barefoot along the tide. I missed her with a desperation that was difficult to understand. So much time had been wasted over the years, but we were taking our first true steps towards our future.

As nightfall cascaded across the city, we made our way towards the center of town for the festival. In honor of St. Joseph, Las Falles was an annual spectacle with burning of wood and papier-mâché sculptures. The most prominent stories in the zeitgeist, pop culture, or the imaginations of the artist were on display in the streets.

While most were only three or four feet tall, many intersections were barricaded and hosted two-story sculptures. It wasn't until later that we understood what the barricades were for: the larger sculptures were filled with fireworks and were set aflame in the middle of the streets!

The endless hours of dancing, laughing, drinking, and visual stimuli were more exciting than I'd ever experienced at one time, and I was glad to leave the city well before the festivities ended. As exhausted as I was, I didn't really mind that everyone else had the opportunity to sleep while I drove home.

As Dayna dozed in the passenger seat, I imagined us as parents taking the kids home from a long day at the fair. The more I thought of the family I would build with the woman sitting next to me, the more alive and awake I felt.

Dayna and I spent my last weeks in Madrid seeing all the sights we'd saved for ourselves. Walks through the Prado or wandering countless parks filled our days. We lunched in promenades and squares while she retold the history she'd learned. I was so happy and fulfilled that I began to rethink my plans of going home.

For far too long, I'd placed things and ego above my love for her. I'd neglected her and not been present at times when she needed me most. We'd lost too many years to miscommunication and temporary dalliances, and I wanted desperately to have that time back. At the very least, we could take the next few months for us before we consigned ourselves to the business of life.

We discussed our next steps late into the evenings. We were torn between our youth and desires to be care-free, the time we'd wasted, and the call of marriage and family. She still needed to graduate and discover a career, while I had a job that I was scheduled to start in a few weeks. Despite our desires in the moment, we knew we couldn't live with regret of the past. We had the rest of our lives to be with each other; building our foundation was the most important thing we could do in the moment.

"Maybe we should get married here in Spain," I said, only half-joking.

"That would be great for us, but everyone would kill us!" she laughed.

"Why?"

"Because! You know everyone wants to be there."

"Why does anyone else matter? You know I don't care how other people feel." We both laughed knowing the full extent of my indifference to other people's feeling.

"I'm not marrying you now," she said; her mood becoming more serious. "To be honest, I'm not sure what I want."

"You don't want to marry me?" I asked, slightly taken aback.

"Of course I do. There are just things I want to do first. I need to find a job and I'm not sure I even want to go back home. You already have a job back home, and I don't know how to deal with that."

There was something in her voice that brought me to attention. For all the hopes and dreams we'd shared over the years, she was getting cold feet.

"Listen, I was just playing. There are things we both need to do. I want to go to grad school at some point. But I do know one thing: I want to be wherever you are. If you don't want to live in California, we don't have to. If you want to live in Spain, I'll move here and learn Spanish, even though I hate it. You are the only thing I ever wanted in life. I'm really just here to help make your dreams come true. Your vision has always been better than mine."

She kissed me deeply as we lay on our bed listening to Jill Scott.

"I just want the opportunity to find myself," she said. "I've lived my whole life under my parents' rules and I need to know who I am if I'm every going to be the wife and mother I want to be. I need to know you support that."

"That's all I ever wanted to do."

We continued this way for several hours. No matter how well we knew each other, there were things we'd never discussed. Some topics were overlooked as a function of our youth, but we had also evolved as people.

With a heavy heart, I left Spain at the end of March. The life we wanted to build would not be easy, but we were committed to building it with each other. We were soulmates; the rest would work itself out. My responsibility was to go home, earn and save money for our first home. Her pending graduation, job search, and re-acclimation to the pace of life would make things hectic when she returned home, but this was the dynamic of our relationship and I was happy to play my part.

Back home, I assimilated quickly into my new job. Although I'd promised I'd never live in my mother's house again, staying home was the most economical situation to save money. It was odd to work for the same company as my mother, but it was even stranger to work in the same building or be recognized by many of the colleagues she'd had since my childhood.

The work wasn't as cutting edge as what I did in Houston, but I was happy with the lower stress level and opportunity to grow in a company I respected and admired. My new team was supportive, and I had an instant rapport with my manager, Ana.

I spoke with Dayna daily. She was almost done with the last of her classes and couldn't wait to be finished. She was intermittently apprehensive of what life would be like after graduation, but all she really wanted was to enjoy the journey and not rush past all the small moments that make life worthwhile.

I was more than a little envious when she called to tell me about her Spring Break plans. A friend from high school was flying over to spend a few weeks and they were going to the southern coast of Spain for a few days. As beautiful as late April was in the Bay Area, the coast of Spain seemed like a better alternative.

She'd called to ask for money to make it all work. I wasn't upset—what was mine was also hers. I only wished that I could be enjoying my money in Spain with her.

"I'm a little jealous of you," I confessed. "I should have stayed in Spain with you."

"But you had a job. What else could you do?"

"I have enough cash from selling my Enron stock. I could have stayed as long as I wanted. I'll be working the rest of my life. I'd rather be with you."

"I know what you mean, baby, but I'll be home in a month. We'll have all the time in the world."

"Ok. I still don't like it, though."

We went on to make plans for me to send the cash, and I

made her promise to catch her bus on time. I didn't have money to waste on missed connections.

"Sure, whatever!" she laughed. "Thank you, babe. I love you. I'll call when I arrive."

Year 24: Part 4 - Rock Bottom

A phone call from Mrs. Gray woke me up in the middle of the night. There had been an accident, she said in a panic. She couldn't get in touch with Dayna. Her friend had called, but the connection was bad.

"Can you help me find out what's going on?"

Assuring her that I'd figure everything out, I called the number she gave me. Before long, I was able to get through to Dayna's friend. Still in shock, she began to recount the events of the evening.

They'd missed their first bus and had taken the night bus on the way to Mallorca. There'd been a light rain, but nothing to be concerned about. In an attempt to pass another vehicle, the bus failed to follow the curve of the road and drove off the embankment, causing a number of injuries. Although she and Dayna had been sitting next to each other, they were separated in the chaos, and she was having trouble getting information because she didn't speak Spanish.

Giving my second assurance of the night, I hung the phone. Not being fluid in Spanish myself, I called a friend from Houston who could translate via a three-way call. She agreed to help, and we made several calls to the authorities in Spain. One call led to several other calls. As we made our way through the maze of information, we were finally placed on a call with the lead medical examiner. I didn't need a translator to confirm my worst fear.

"She's dead, mama."

My composure threatened to crumble as my mother's wail of despair pierced the air. It was all that I could do to keep myself from succumbing to the void enveloping the corners of my mind. There was too much work to be done and I needed her help. I didn't have the capacity to help her keep her shit together.

There would be time to grieve later. My mother was my rock, and I needed her to give me stability because the difficult parts were still ahead: I needed to tell Dayna's parents that their daughter would not be coming home.

The morning sun was unnaturally bright as phone calls were made. Informing everyone was a steadying force—something firm to lean against as I clung to my last vestiges of composure. By this time, Matt had arrived and Bryan was close behind him. There was nothing more for me to do and I needed air, so my mother cautiously let me leave with them.

As we drove to Fremont to pick up JaDaun, my mind would partially focus on a thought before it was snatched away. I was barely aware of the events happening around me as I was shuttled from one location to the next. At some point, I found myself walking up the incline of Strawberry Canyon surrounded by my friends.

I couldn't focus on anything except walking up the hill. My body felt numb and ill-fitting. The midmorning had become warm as the sun continued its inexorably journey across the clear, blue sky. Looking out from the hillside, the waters of the bay glistened like diamonds. The preternatural beauty seemed to mock the void that danced at the corners of my sight.

Feeling increasingly tired, I stopped on a plateau to rest. *Only for a moment: you have to keep moving*, I thought. The darkness in my peripheral vision had found a comfortable place to settle as I tried to breathe. The next breath was tougher, and the next tougher still. My ears were pounding as the sound of my beating heart joined into the chorus of shock threatening to overtake me. I started to cry.

The pain was too much to bear. For every sob that was able to escape, there were two more to take its place. It wasn't just the loss of Dayna I was mourning—I had lost an entire life. Gone were holiday dinners, birthdays, the children we would have, and the smell of their hair as they slept—so much like their mother's. All of the people I would have known and became close with and loved—they were gone with her. All of it was lost before I'd had a chance to find it with her.

I was suffocating under the weight of grief and was slowly being overcome by fear. I feared the emptiness would consume me and never let go. Living with this pain was too much to comprehend. I wanted it all to end—pain, grief, anger. All of it.

In that moment, one thought was clear: I wanted to die.

I stood on that cliff knowing I could jump and my pain would end. The seduction of the freedom it promised was hard to resist. In a moment of hesitation, however, I was saved. Not by the voice of Jesus or angels dispatched to rescue me. It was something far more basic and human: anger and hatred.

Year 24: Part 5 - Left Behind

Death comes for us all and we are powerless to resist it when it is our time. Dayna's time had come, and she was able to transcend to the next phase. Whatever her state, she was done with this world and her story was complete. For all of the pain and grief, I knew my story was just beginning.

It was difficult to *be* in those first few days. There was a strong desire to retreat into the darkness. I welcomed the support of my friends and family, but I also wanted to be alone so that I could release the despair that was never far from breaking through the stoic façade I had constructed.

I'd attempted to go back to work the day after I'd found out, but barely an hour had passed before the unimportance of it was too much to tolerate. A leave of absence was requested and granted.

I could see the worry on my mother's face. She had lost someone she loved deeply, but she had a responsibility to be present for me. I'm not sure what she was thinking or feeling, but she refused to leave me alone for too long those first days. I loved her for it, but I also wished she would leave me to whatever fate had in store for me.

When we visited Dayna's family to work on the logistics of bringing her body back and funeral planning, I made sure one of my boys was close by to take me away when the pressure became too much. Her parents' house was frequented by well-wishers stopping by to extend their condolences. Their faces eventually faded into an avatar of grief and sadness that threatened to coax my own into a dramatic appearance.

After losing my composure a few times, I resolved to avoid their house as much as possible. I was thankful for the respite my friends provided, but even they became too much. It was increasingly difficult to maintain a semblance of sanity.

Play nice, be the stoic soldier, and I'll let you have a moment to release it all, the voice in my head assured me. *If you lose your shit in front of everyone, they'll all fall apart. You have to be strong for everyone else.*

I could feel myself slipping away and I didn't have the strength to fight it any longer. I needed to be alone with my grief. I assured friends and family I would be okay, even though I knew a breakdown was coming.

When I was finally alone, I gave myself permission to have a moment. Not too long, lest I lose myself completely. As I stood in the kitchen, waiting for anguish to consume me, I was interrupted by the house phone ringing. When I heard the voice on the line, I nearly dropped the phone in shock: it was Sancho.

Sancho and I had never been friends. We had mutual friends, had known each other for nearly a decade and attended the same college, but we were far from friendly. We weren't exactly enemies, but there was little love lost.

"How are you doing?" he asked.

"I'm good, man. What's up?"

"Yeah, dude. I heard about your girl and I wanted to tell you I'm sorry for you."

"Thanks, dude," I replied hurriedly.

"We've had our differences, but you've always been a good dude. When Remy told me what happened, I wanted to reach out to you. We've grown up together, went to Morehouse together, and I consider you a brother. If you need anything, I'm here for you."

"Wow. I really appreciate that. You don't know how much this means to me."

In my moment of anguish and distress, I was shown empathy and compassion by a man I largely despised. Sancho's call made the pain slightly easier to manage. He was the last person I'd ever imagined hearing from, but I was grateful for him. The love he extended was a light in the darkness. I may have hated God, but through God, my friend Sancho showed me grace.

It was interesting to watch the pattern I was succumbing to. It's hard to describe the sensation of losing one's mind to grief while observing and cataloging the experience. It was like experiencing the most vivid dream you could ever have. I could feel the physical sensation of anguish in my body, but my consciousness was a separate thing. I was two people in one body: one to feel, the other to think.

It was through Dayna's death that I began to understand the nature of my life. My grief wasn't the result of her death, it was triggered by it. I immersed myself in it in order to understand a fundamental truth: I grieved not because Dayna was dead, but because *I was alive.*

I wanted to wake up to her every morning and kiss her before I fell asleep. I wanted to hold her hand, make love to her, and smell her hair. I wanted her wisdom, support, and vision to guide the path of my life. The loss was the source of anguish and I didn't want to live the rest of my life without those things. The depths of my pain were a testament to the depths of my love.

Her spirit would always be with me. She had taught me the entirety of what she could, and it was my time to take those lessons to the next level. I had to learn to live for myself. If I truly loved her, my mandate would be to live life to the fullest and be the man she always wished me to be.

Year 25: Part 1 - Adrift

My friends became indispensable to me. They had carried me over the roughest waters of my life and I was eternally grateful. Though I was close with all of my brothers, my relationship with Tehran expanded in ways that I never foresaw. We'd been friends at Morehouse, but naturally I hadn't been as close to him as I'd been with Remy and Jabari with whom I grew up with.

Tehran and I settled into a routine of weekly hikes and brunch to discuss the events of the previous week. In him, I found a kindred spirit who was also plagued by questions more existential than topical. There was no happenstance in our world; all things were interconnected, and we were keen to slowly unravel the mysteries we observed. More than anyone, he was the lodestar keeping me on the path of reason and understanding.

The rest of my time was spent getting high, partying, and seeking out the company of women. Without malice, I used them for whatever they had to offer. Some were simply friends I leaned on, while other relationships were sexual in nature. I never lied to anyone, but I know I wasn't always open with my thoughts and feelings. I did, however, love everyone for their uniqueness and the value they brought to my life.

Ehren was a perfect example of someone whose friendship I came to cherish in those days. After Dayna's death, she was one of the first people to call. She made sure to stay in contact in the weeks and months following that ordeal. Although she was out of state, she let me know I was never far from her thoughts and prayers.

While we didn't start as friends when we met in Houston, the years that followed saw a thaw in our relationship. She was a good person, and I admitted that I was probably more of an asshole to her than she'd deserved in those early days. We were able to laugh about it and develop a good friendship, in spite of foolishness of our younger selves. So when her birthday arrived and all of her friends backed out of their trip to Los Angeles, I encouraged her to keep her trip and I would fly down to meet her.

Her birthday was the perfect excuse for me to do something impulsive and off-script. In a convertible red Mustang, we cruised the city taking in the sights and sounds of a beautiful summer weekend. From Hollywood to the beach, from the Valley to South Central, we were young people living life and enjoying it. It was one of the first moments of real happiness I experienced since I'd been with Dayna in Spain.

There were also the countless women I had meaningless flings with who helped distract me. When I was bored of the women I met around Oakland, I became an early adopter of internet dating. From random cities in the Bay Area to Los Angeles, I had a series of affairs that served no purpose but to artificially boost my fragile ego and sense of self-worth. *This is what young men are supposed to do*, I rationalized.

Somewhere in the middle of my philandering, I met Melanie—a cute redhead with a mess of freckles and a sly smile. She and I had caught each other's eye at a club one night after a group of us had traveled to Sacramento to hang with Remy. I wasn't used to having anyone look at me the way she did, but I was in no hurry to talk her out of it.

The more I got to know her, the more she intrigued me. She was French Canadian, from a small town in Quebec, and had lived in Sacramento for a number of years. A scientist by trade, she had a quick and curious mind that was extremely attractive. It was nothing for me to drive the hundred miles from my house in Oakland to her place north of Sacramento.

Our relationship didn't last, however. The longer we saw each other, the more uneasy I became. I couldn't identify the source of my discomfort, but it grew the more I wondered why we were even dating.

I never invited her to Oakland or made arrangements for her to meet my friends. Most of our time was spent alone with each other. Could it be because she was white? Perhaps I simply didn't like her any more than I did, I reasoned.

I wasn't racist, but my increasing ambivalence towards building a relationship with her troubled me. I knew in my heart that I didn't care about her race, but I did question it. We ended it shortly after.

After Melanie, I met Karen. She'd been friends with Bryan and JaDaun in high school, but we'd never met for some reason. When Bryan called one day and said Karen needed help moving into her new apartment, I didn't hesitate.

In my opinion, the mark of a true friend is one that will help you move, and any friend of Bryan and JaDaun was a friend of mine. When we arrived in Stockton and she opened the door, I was smitten. Her dark brown skin, full lips and friendly eyes made her look like an exotic princess.

Karen and I never gave a name to what we were doing. It was arbitrary and unnecessary, and she didn't seem to mind. We were friends is all anyone needed to know. There was no jealousy or possessiveness: all of us would frequently go to clubs or lounges and we were free to talk to and flirt with anyone that caught our eye.

Despite this unspoken agreement, there was never a time I didn't leave with the same people I arrived with. As far as I was concerned, leaving with her couldn't be bested. We did have one moment of awkwardness, however.

Waking up one morning, I thought nothing of cooking my favorite breakfast for her. I loved cooking. The ancient alchemy of creating nourishment for people I cared for gave me a lot of satisfaction. Most of my friends knew this and were more than enthusiastic to accept this gift from me. Of all the things I knew how to cook, scrambled eggs were my favorite. It took me years to perfect what I would consider perfect fluffy eggs. It was frustrating and amazing that something so simple was so difficult to make right.

A few days later, Bryan pulled me aside and mentioned that there was an issue with Karen that I needed to address. She was aware of the Dayna situation and was wary of me falling in love with her so quickly. Slightly annoyed but mostly amused, I told him I would take care of it. He knew what I was about and tried to explain it to her, but she was unsure.

As I explained the benign gesture of cooking for her, she was skeptical but eventually accepted my explanation. We dated for a few more months, but that conversation lingered with me when I did begin to entertain the possibility of having more with her.

She was beautiful, funny, and a very good friend, but I was hesitant to lose her in an attempt to add a weight our relationship couldn't bear. We decided our friendship was too important to lose and mutually decided to end our romantic encounters.

Shaina was a more complicated situation. I'd been friends with her since high school. I'd dated a good friend of hers and she dated Jabari for a time. Even if I wanted to date her, "guy code" demanded fealty into perpetuity.

Our relationship eventually turned into something more substantial than a physical relationship could provide. Slowly and steadily, she became one of my closest confidants. With her, I could open up and explore my emotional side in ways I couldn't with Melanie, Karen, or random girls I kept company with. We would joke that it was the combination of my Virgo and her Pieces signs. I didn't bother to understand it, but I was grateful for her company.

The more time I spent with her, the more I thought about being with her. She drove me crazy at times with her over-the-top emotionality, but it was also the source of her fire and passion. No matter what my heart desired, my sense of honor and loyalty were paramount. As we both cycled through failed relationships, I secretly wished I could show her how she deserved to be loved.

Year 25: Part 2 –
No Time to Be Afraid

On a beautiful Tuesday morning, I silenced my 7 a.m. alarm and climbed out of bed. It was the kind of day that makes going to work difficult. I took a quick shower, brushed my teeth, and returned to my room to get dressed. I turned on the television to check the forecast and realized that it was going to be a dark day: the towers in New York were on fire.

By the time I tuned in, the idea that this was a major terrorist attack was a certainty. I was mesmerized by the images on my screen; the carnage and misery of the human condition weighing heavy on my mind. I thought of all the families joining the tragic club I'd found myself a member of after Dayna's death. Even as the thoughts of what those people were going through filled my mind, I felt nothing. There were no emotions or break in my morning routine. This was life, I reasoned.

The train was silent as it collected passengers on their journey into San Francisco. The weight of the morning's events hung heavily in the air precluding the need for conversation. I'd witnessed several historic events in my life: the Challenger explosion, the fall of the Berlin Wall, the stock crash of 1987, but nothing compared to the impact this event was having.

There was a palpable sense of danger and foreboding. Was our country and way of life over? And why in the hell was I commuting into a major city center while terrorists were actively targeting such places?

When I arrived at my building I was confronted by security personnel insisting everyone leave the premises. Although there were people currently inside, they had received orders to place the building on lockdown.

When we were allowed to return to work a few days later, I was shocked to find that my absence was a point of contention with my director. He and a few of my colleagues had been in the office when the news broke, and while he understood we couldn't enter the building, he had an issue with my absence on a hastily convened conference call. I brushed the matter off until I found myself summoned to his office with my manager in tow.

Once seated, he began to lecture me on my absence and failure to conform to the team. The more he talked, the angrier I became. The arrogance of this man to lecture me in the midst of a national crisis was beyond anything I'd ever experienced.

"Do you have anything to say?" he asked smugly.

"Was there work to be done?" I asked.

"That's not the point!" he retorted. "The whole team was on the call. You should have been there."

"I didn't think it was a big deal at the time."

He continued his lecture as my patience quickly waned.

"Do you have a problem with my work?" I challenged.

"Your work has been fine."

"So what's the problem?"

He was shocked that I had the audacity to speak to him as an equal. What he failed to understand was that the white man I'd previously worked for had exhausted my tolerance for that type of treatment. Maybe it wasn't a black and white thing, but I wasn't in the mood to figure it out. The optics didn't look right. Coupled with my continued state of emotional barrenness, I had zero fucks to give him and his ego.

"Your work is fine. That's not the issue. This is an 'at-will' position, however."

There it is! That's the threat you've been waiting to use on me.

"I know it's 'at-will'. I also know that I can quit any time I want."

My manager, Ana, shifted uncomfortably in her seat as he and I stared each other down. From the look on his face, he seemed perplexed as to what to do next. I knew he didn't really want to escalate this any further; his wasn't a defensible position in light of a national tragedy.

"Are we done?"

"Yes," he said wearily.

I should have quit then and there. I was tired of being disrespected by people seeking to keep me in my place. I was beginning to understand that I had a unique way of seeing things. This was a talent that needed to be nurtured, not stifled and subjugated. Only a few months on the job, and I knew this stop was best kept short.

The truth is, I was afraid of the unknown. Despite the savings I'd acquired and my confidence in finding another job, I was afraid to quit without having something else lined up. Besides, quitting would make me no better than the stereotypical black man, unable to hold down a job.

The specter of my father's inability to provide for the family in a consistent manner haunted me. My vow to always earn superseded all other desires. How I felt about it was inconsequential. I was already living at home with my mother; I couldn't also be unemployed. Besides, my tastes were too expensive to not have steady income.

Luckily, I had an opportunity to visit my sister in Germany. Another reason I couldn't quit—international travel without a job would have been the height of irresponsibility. Shortly before I'd left Houston, Naima and Kevin were transferred to Germany to complete their next enlistment assignment. Very soon after relocating, we were blessed with the news that she was expecting their first child. In celebration, my mother and I planned to fly over to attend the birth of my nephew.

On a personal level, making the trip to Germany would be in honor of Dayna and keeping her spirit alive. It wasn't lost on me that she died living life to its fullest. Some people die after painful fights with cancer, some die simply walking in the neighborhood they'd lived in their entire life. Dayna died in love, exploring a foreign land en route to her next great adventure. There were few better ways to depart this world than under those circumstances.

I was far more excited for Germany than it was worth. While it was a charming town, Darmstadt didn't offer the level of excitement I was looking for. Despite its locale on the other side of the world, it wasn't much different than a typical Midwest town of equal size. The abundance of U.S. military installations and personnel further degraded its appeal. Seeking greater adventure on my first night, I borrowed my sister's car and drove the half-hour to Frankfurt.

The night started on an inauspicious note when I attempted to fill up the car before the trip. Secure in my currency conversion estimate, I started the pump and returned to the driver's seat. When the pump stopped, I exited the car and was shocked. I'd spent nearly $70 for fifteen gallons!

It had to be a mistake. Irritated and determined to resolve the issue, I approached the attendant in order to plead my case hoping he knew enough English to facilitate a productive exchange.

I contemplated my argument as I waited on the person in front of me to finish their transaction. The longer I waited, however, the more I was unsure of my position. Something wasn't adding up, but I couldn't figure out what was wrong. Then I realized my mistake: the price was listed in liters, not gallons. I hoped my trip to the city was worth the exorbitant price I'd paid.

Sadly, the night didn't improve. Frankfurt was no Madrid. The bustling nightlife I was expecting was nowhere to be found. All I was able to find was Frankfurt's red-light district and a semi-empty bar, where I decided to have a drink.

The bartender informed me that Frankfurt didn't have much nightlife. I was more likely to find a cool party back in Darmstadt. The only interesting thing to happen in Frankfurt was my inadvertent discovery of a heroin dispensary, complete with a crowd of junkies loitering on the street.

Undeterred in my quest to make my vacation memorable, I began to plan a more elaborate excursion. Naima's due date was only a week away, so I didn't want to travel too far. I narrowed my options to two cities: Amsterdam and Prague. I told Naima and she informed me her entire platoon was banned from Amsterdam because of the trouble they'd caused—exactly the type of weekend I was looking for.

I arrived in Amsterdam with little incident. I found a hotel and within another twenty minutes I was exploring the city. By happenstance, my hotel was situated on a quiet street on the outskirts of the red-light district. Intrigued, I walked along the canals, taking in the sights of legalized vice.

A variety of sex workers sat casually on the other side of large windows for potential patrons to review. Highlighted by the pinkish-red lights framing the windows, many posed seductively while others occupied themselves by reading various types of literature. I couldn't discern if I was perplexed by the juxtaposition of a reading prostitute or the fact that they read at all.

Sex workers were the second most notorious aspect of Amsterdam. The only thing left was to find a suitable place to partake in the first: legal marijuana. I noticed several promising establishments and walked into the nearest one. The soft, welcoming light was betrayed by the harsh melodies of heavy metal music playing over the sound system. Smoking to metal music held no appeal. I left without making a purchase.

Walking along the canal, I discovered a coffee shop with a Jamaican flag in the window. Taking it as a sign of a much cooler vibe, I walked in to survey. With Bob Marley playing in the background, I sat at an empty table and reviewed the menu. But like Goldilocks, I didn't find this shop to be any more suitable than the first. Smoking to reggae seemed too much of a cliché, so I left in search of something better.

Further down the canal, I found a shop playing a nice mix of down tempo lounge music that was more to my liking. Taking a seat, I reviewed the menu of various marijuana strains and hashish, amazed at the diversity of choice. Not sure how to choose, I settled on Bubble Gum for no other reason than to taste bubble gum in my weed.

I rolled a joint, lit it, and took a long drag before I sipped my sparkling water. Although everything I was doing was legal, it was hard to shake the feelings of nervousness. It wasn't much different than being in California, aside from the use of a register to purchase it. Underwhelmed, I left the shop in search of an experience along the canals.

Instead of feeling better, I felt progressively worse. I was very high, but the feeling of paranoia wasn't due to the marijuana. The pimps, prostitutes, and various stag parties along the canal made me feel especially conspicuous. My camera and style of dress marked me as a tourist and a potential target. For the first time in a long time, I felt fear.

As the weekend progressed, my fear lingered. After venturing further into Amsterdam and away from the debauchery of the red-light district, it subsided slightly but remained present. The more I contemplated my fear and anxiety, the more I realized I lacked the confidence that had carried me thus far through life.

Despite my ability to function day to day, I was hurting with no idea how to make it better. I was afraid to desire happiness, because I feared it would be stolen from me. As life endured around me, I took the first mental steps on what I knew would be a long journey of rediscovery.

Year 25: Part 3 – Complications

Despite the sense of fear and anxiety I'd suffered, Amsterdam had been good for me. I came home with a renewed sense of confidence, ready to reestablish the normal course of my life.

One of the changes I'd decided to make was to pursue an MBA. I knew I wanted more out of life, and enhancing my knowledge and gaining new skills was going to be my gateway to the existence I envisioned so many years before. Even though I was unhappy with my current position at work, it provided the stability I needed to plan my next step. As soon as I was back to work, I scheduled a meeting with Fritz, my new director.

Fritz and I always had a friendly relationship, so I assumed he would support my decision. But my request was met with condescension. He couldn't justify allocating budget for me to pursue my MBA and ended the meeting just as quickly as it had started. I realized Fritz was just another white man taking the license to pass judgment on me and the station he believed I should occupy. Unfazed by his attempt to derail me, I initiated another transfer.

Later that summer, I went to Houston to attend a wedding for my friend Steve, someone Reg and I had hung out with frequently when I worked at Enron. Even though it had only been a year and a half, it felt like a lifetime ago. I couldn't even recognize the Rahmaan I had been during that time.

Shortly after I arrived, I met up with Reg. We both needed to buy wedding gifts, so we made the familiar trip to the Galleria. As we laughed at the adventures we'd had in that city and the crazy things that had happened since, we both marveled at how strange it was to be marrying off a friend at twenty-six years old. We weren't young, but we certainly felt odd recognizing we were at an age where marriage was becoming common.

After we finished shopping, we went to Steve's house for a dinner he and his fiancé, Shimona, were hosting. There was a lot of food, card games, and good-natured joking to keep us all entertained.

In between the jokes, there was a particular laugh that caught my attention. It was bright and lively, followed by a sweet voice with a distinct southern inflection. Stacey moved through the party, commanding the room with her presence. She was cute and nearly as tall as me, though not exactly my type. I normally dated girls much shorter, but there was a familiarity about her.

As the weekend progressed, I made sure to be wherever she was. When the wedding party rendezvoused at the resort the night before the wedding, I sought her out. When the guys weren't able to spend our bachelor night in Lake Charles due to the couple's last minute cold feet, I wasn't unhappy that I had more opportunity to spend with her. Being near her was increasingly more important to me—so much so that I made sure we kept in touch after the wedding.

We began a ritual of calling each other every night. Originally from Atlanta, she'd moved to Kansas City a few years earlier to live with her parents while she attended graduate school. The more I talked to her, the more I looked forward to our evening calls. These revolved around her nightly visit to the gym, and it wasn't uncommon to hear her getting a few miles in on the treadmill. Her work as a managed child care director and studies to obtain her master's degree was a major draw for me. I thought she was amazing. Very quickly, our friendly calls turned into something much more.

We both understood the difficulties surrounding long-distance relationships and decided to visit each other on a regular schedule. Every three weeks or so, she would visit California. I visited her family a couple of times in Kansas City, but she preferred to visit California due to the wealth of activities. When we visited Atlanta for Thanksgiving, making a stop by Steve's parent's home for a gathering of friends, everyone was surprised that we were a couple. Though everyone genuinely wished us well, it was a shock nonetheless.

Though we came from different backgrounds, I found myself falling in love with her. It wasn't a seamless fit, which was obvious in the surprise from others, but the budding affection between us was solid. Despite all of our differences, including our religious views, we both seemed to want more from life than what we had. And we got along well enough.

So, it seemed natural to ask her to move to California with me. She was rapidly approaching graduation without a definitive plan except that she wanted to leave Kansas City. The distance between Kansas City and Oakland was manageable for a short time. My experience attempting a long-distance relationship with Dayna, however, made me certain that Stacey and I wouldn't survive much longer.

Though I'm sure it wasn't unexpected, Stacey still seemed surprised at my offer. We'd only dated for a few months and it was a big step at this stage in our relationship. Her reservations were shared by many of my friends when I revealed my idea to them. I was aware of what I was offering and what it would mean for the relationship I was cultivating. I'd thought long and hard about what I wanted my life to be, and I felt confident that the road I was choosing would lead to happiness—even if it wasn't the vision I'd held for so long.

Despite asking Stacey to move in with me, I was still mostly indifferent. My cavalier attitude had almost nothing to do with Stacey and more to do with a growing certainty that I was simply on the ride provided by life. I knew I was powerless to control destiny, but I had no fear of whatever misfortune might befall me. I'd already been to the bottom.

Once Stacey agreed to move in with me, she eagerly finished her last few weeks of school and began packing her belongings. Our plan was to drive from Kansas City back to Oakland, arriving home in time for Christmas with my mother and her new husband. To prepare for our new life together, we traded in Stacey's sports car for an SUV. Even though I still felt like I was simply existing in my life, our love was tangible and the journey we were about to embark on was exciting.

The move to bring her from KC to Oakland was smooth; she was able to transfer her job to a local site south of San Francisco, eliminating the hassle of a job search. Our only task was to familiarize her with the area and develop a living routine.

The first few weeks went well. We had a few rough patches, but nothing out of the ordinary. The stress was to be expected, considering that we were getting used to living with each other and she was in a new city. And though I knew she had fears of relocating, she acclimated nicely and was excited for the next step in our relationship. Nothing, however, could have prepared us for how much our life was about to change.

"I'm late," she told me one evening.

I wasn't worried. From what I understood, women were always a day or so off from time to time. The past few weeks, while fun, were incredibly stressful and that most likely was the reason, I rationalized. She was adamant and wouldn't rest until the she took a test.

Slightly annoyed, I got dressed and drove to the store. It took a while to find one I felt was suitable, but I returned home with several boxes of pregnancy tests. Handing her the packages, I returned to the show I was watching and settled back in for the evening. She appeared in the doorway a few minutes later with panic in her eyes.

"I'm PREGNANT!" She was in a near panic. I was in denial, not ready to believe her.

"Let me see that," I said, gesturing to the test. I looked at the stick with the double pink lines on it. Even then, I still didn't want to believe it. I decided to create a control sample with the other stick. Jabari worked for a company that specialized in those types of tests and he'd told me that men could generate false positives for a variety of reasons including prostate cancer. After a few minutes, I exited the bathroom as cold reality poured over me.

"Well, the good news is, I don't have prostate cancer," I laughed weakly.

Year 26: When Things Gets Real

I wasn't ready to be a father. I wasn't sure if I even wanted kids. Although I'd considered having kids with Dayna, that was more out of love and devotion to her rather than a desire of my own. Stacey and I were still a new couple and the thought of having a child under those circumstances scared me. The idea of having an abortion wasn't any easier to digest, despite the pro-choice leanings I may have harbored. The one thing I was certain of, however, was that I was no longer in control of my life's path.

"So…what were your thoughts about it?" I offered deferentially. This wasn't the time for me to offer unvarnished opinions.

"I'm not having an abortion if that's what you're thinking!"

"OK, but we have to consider every option," I said in the most soothing tone I could muster.

"Abortion is never an option!"

"So what do you think we should do?" I asked, already resigned to our fate. She fumbled through her words nervously, but eventually settled on the one idea that would make everything palatable in her mind.

"What about getting married?"

"Absolutely not! That is a terrible reason to get married," I said.

As far as I was concerned, marriage was out of the question. It may have been ironic to use the brevity of our relationship as my primary excuse, but it happened to be true. It was too soon in our relationship to discuss marriage—even with the strong possibility of fatherhood in nine months.

Though I was against getting married, I did promise her that I would take care of her and our child, no matter what.

Over the next few days we began the process of informing our families and friends. The situation was much too serious for the customary first trimester waiting period. We needed help and support, and no amount of anxiety or uncertainty was more important than that.

Telling my family and friends wasn't the most comfortable conversation, but I shared the news with little trouble. The people closest to me had recently witnessed me at my worse and there was no more room for shame or secrecy in my life. Stacey's conversations were more difficult for her.

I sensed a fair amount of shame as she revealed the turn of events to her parents. She was unwed and pregnant by someone she'd only known for six months—it wasn't supposed to be her path. Her parents weren't happy about it, and despite her assurance that I was going to take care of her, I'm sure they had their reservations.

I couldn't blame them—I was disappointed in myself. I'd worked my entire life to not be in this exact situation, but there I was. Despite my education, age, and career achievements, I'd still knocked up a girl I'd just started dating. My fear of fatherhood added to my disappointment. I still had too many issues within myself that I hadn't solved. My greatest worry was bringing a child into the world and failing them because of my inadequacies.

It felt as if everything in the world was as unhinged as I was in those days. The various conflicts in the Middle East were in ascendancy due to the terror attacks a few months earlier. With my sister and brother-in-law on active duty, the rising storm threatened to cause permanent damage to my family. Kevin was deployed to Iraq almost immediately, while my sister was on-call to be deployed at a later time. In response to these orders, it was determined that it would be best if my nephew, Elijah, lived with us in California until the situation with my sister was more certain.

Elijah's presence brought a measure of calm to me. He was just shy of his first birthday, and it felt like a test run of things to come. He wasn't a fussy baby and he brought a playful energy to the house. As I wrestled with Elijah on the floor, mirroring the games and playfulness my father showed me all those years ago, a certain amount of tension was slowly released. *I might be okay at this after all,* I thought.

Not too long after he arrived, Naima received confirmation that she would not be deployed. The news came earlier than I'd expected, and though we were relieved, I couldn't help feeling melancholy about Elijah going back to Germany. In his brief time with us, I'd found a measure of purpose. I was sad, but I understood the gift of that time for what it was: to assure me that I was more prepared for fatherhood than I thought.

My mother was supposed to take Elijah back, but she had a scheduling conflict so the trip fell to me. Stacey wasn't happy about it, but I needed the break. Too many things had occurred in too short a time, and the time away would help me prepare for the arrival of my own child.

After returning Elijah back to Naima, I made plans for an excursion to the Czech Republic. For nearly a year, I'd regretted my decision to visit Amsterdam over Prague and I was motivated to make amends. To my disappointment, however, I missed the last direct train to Prague by seconds (German trains are stringently punctual). Determined to maximize this grand adventure, I caught the first train east with an overnight connection in Dresden. Anywhere was better than staying still.

Arriving in Dresden late into the evening, I took a long, slow breath. The cool air seemed to calm the fires of anxiety that had become all too familiar in my chest. Despite the long international flight, the additional train ride, and the many hours of missed sleep, I was surprisingly energized. I'd heard the story of Dresden and the devastation caused in World War II, but it was still here. There was a monument of historic buildings to commemorate the past, but all around it was a city of the present and future.

After a night of partying, I boarded the first train to Prague. I couldn't explain why, but my excitement was growing. It felt as if I was being pulled to the city and I was eager to find out why. I had no specific plans and knew very little about the city, yet it was a place that I needed to see. It would have the answers to questions I couldn't articulate.

Stepping out of the train station, I walked to the corner and glanced around. I had no place to go and it felt wonderful. For the first time in a long time, my steps would be in pursuit of my own desires and not in service of someone else. I didn't even have a place to sleep that night, but that detail only underscored the sense of adventure I was experiencing. Noticing another traveler, I started a conversation, quickly making a friend, and made arraignments to lodge at a hostel he recommended.

The next few days were an intoxicating mix of history, partying, strippers, and absinthe. Prague, a city untouched by the ravages of war, was a pristine monument to a thousand years of architectural wonder. Its warren of cobbled streets, hidden doors, and sun baked terra-cotta shingles were the manifestation of a fairytale come to life.

By day I explored the city, getting lost in the streets and my dreams and thoughts. At night, the city cloaked our crew of hostel compatriots in shadows and fog to better hide our mischief and misdeeds. All the while, the absinthe flowed, helping to liberate us from our many inhibitions. My own inhibitions and fears of the life that lay ahead of me, however, were far too powerful to be conquered with alcohol and partying.

When my time in Prague had expired, I boarded a train headed west to Germany and towards real life. I knew these carefree moments were temporary at best, but their loss was deeply felt. As the train pulled out of the station and traced the path of the Vltava River, I felt a tear escape the corner of my eye. As welcoming as the city had been, I knew my pain had nothing to do with Prague. I was losing control over the direction of my life and I was powerless to stop it.

Returning home, I was saddened to realize that my vacation had the opposite effect than I'd intended. Gone were the feelings inspired by Elijah, replaced by a deepening sense of depression. My mood was a mix of ambivalence and dread at my pending fatherhood. Stacey and I were OK, but I was not; fatherhood was something I was accepting, not looking forward to. I wasn't ready, and I wasn't sure how to prepare. The only thing I could do was get through the day at hand. As the weeks and months passed, I knew I needed to make a change.

While it may not have been the most uplifting way to manage life, it was effective. Each day I tried to look at the world through fresh eyes, taking in the beauty and grace offered and not that which I coveted. I looked at Stacey with those same eyes and appreciated the love she had for me and me for her. We were a family bringing new life into the world. We were creating a miracle and it was a privilege to experience it, regardless of the pain.

The day we were to learn our baby's gender was an exciting one. Although I'd never had a strong personal desire for children, I knew that I always wanted a girl. Some thought it strange that I didn't want a son to carry on my name. Others were inadvertently insulting when they questioned the ability of a daughter to carry the family's legacy. *That's exactly why I want a daughter,* I mused. *You'll never see her coming until it's too late.*

Applying gel to Stacey's stomach, the technician engaged us in small talk. She was pleasant enough, but I wasn't here for conversation. Consulting the monitor, she proceeded through her protocols. Although I was preoccupied with my child's gender, there were a number of markers that needed to be checked in order to confirm the baby's health and progress. It wasn't until the end of the exam that she revealed what I already knew in my heart: we were having a daughter.

A feeling of warmth grew in the pit of my stomach and

radiated through my core. It gradually crept into my mind and back down into my throat as I let out a muffled hoot of joy. The tech smiled; I'm sure this was a scene she'd seen hundreds of times but was still amused by it. I hugged and kissed Stacey, before ignoring her chastisement and the sign saying no calls were to be made from the examination room. This joy was too much to have for my own; it had to be shared. I called my mother.

With a renewed sense of optimism, I looked at my life and saw that it was good. I was a twenty-six-year-old homeowner, I had a good job, and I was having a beautiful healthy baby. Although the circumstances weren't perfect, I understood that my acceptance of it could be. I loved my girl, and I was learning to appreciate my life.

Despite caring little for tradition, I still felt it important not to bring a child into the world outside of wedlock. I didn't care, but I knew that society would judge her regardless. Any misgivings I may have had about getting married paled in comparison to the obligation I felt to give her the best life possible.

I surprised Stacey one day at her office. I realized it was a terrible place to ask someone to marry you—the beige walls and fluorescent lights bathed us in sterility that contrasted with the romance of my gesture.

"You know how much I love you, right?" I asked her.

"Yes."

"And I know a lot of things have happened, but I'm feel much better about everything."

"OK," she replied, perplexed. I was bungling this proposal— the look of confusion on her face was my confirmation.

"What I'm trying to say is that I love you. I'm happy to be having a baby with you. Will you marry me?"

The look of shock and love on her face is one I'll always remember. In that moment, she was the most beautiful woman I'd ever seen.

The next few weeks were full of planning. We didn't have much time before the due date and the last-minute decision to get married severely curtailed our options. Neither one of us cared for an elaborate event, so we settled on a brief ceremony overlooking a beautiful cove in Monterrey Bay. Our guest list was small and intimate; only immediate family was in attendance.

A short ceremony followed by an intimate dinner sealed our relationship in matrimony. The setting sun bathed us in the warmth of its gold and crimson light as we dined and toasted the evening away. For all the turmoil that preceded it, my wedding day to Stacey was one that I would always remember fondly.

The day after our wedding, however, was less than ideal.

"What did you want to do today, baby?" she asked.

"I'm not sure. I haven't thought about it. I figured we'd just hang out, maybe get something to eat in town."

"I was thinking of taking my mother down to the beach. They're leaving tomorrow, and she won't have another time to see the ocean."

"What does that have to do with me?" This didn't feel right.

"I was thinking I can go to the beach with my mother and sister while you, my father and brother go play golf. The Del Monte course downstairs is a historic one. They'd love to play it before leaving."

"That's not what I had in mind. I don't even like golf like

that; you know that. I really just want to spend time with you."

"I know, but my mother loves the ocean. She doesn't get to see much of it living in Kansas City. We'll have dinner later. Please?"

Why is her living in the middle of nowhere my problem, I thought. *This isn't what I want.*

I was faced with a dilemma: I could be insistent upon what I wanted, or I could bury my feelings and give this concession to her.

Happy wife, happy life, I reminded myself.

"Sure, fine. Go enjoy the day with your mother," I relented.

"Thanks, babe!" The kiss she gave me, sweet though it was, wasn't enough to mask the slight feelings of bitterness. This marriage thing wasn't starting off the way I'd hoped.

On the morning of September 10th, 2003, we awoke knowing that, from henceforth, we would be charged with the most awesome responsibility in the world. The morning air was cool, belaying the full strength of the heatwave oppressing the city. My wife, absentmindedly rubbing the ring I'd place on her hand roughly two months before, glowed with anticipation of bringing life into the world. Her only concerned seemed to be meeting her self-imposed deadline of 11:59pm so as not to gift her child the birthday of 9/11.

Checking in shortly after 5:00 a.m., we settled into the birthing room with nothing to do but wait. Because of a pending vacation by our doctor, we had scheduled this day for our delivery as illustrated by the Pitocin drip overhanging the bed. This was modern childbirth for the well-to-do, I thought amusingly. While not affluent per se, our insurance was robust enough to accommodate our desire for scheduled childbirth in a private room and a two-day recovery. Thinking of the various levels of care that were possible, I accepted that I was, perhaps, more prepared for being a parent than I gave myself credit for.

Aside from the occasional contraction, there wasn't much for us to do. My mother arrived, soon followed by Stacey's parents. We talked about everything and nothing in an attempt to pass time. The in-room television helped, but there was a lot of nothing to do. As the day progressed, we were joined by our parents as an army of nurses attended to the various monitors and sensors placed around my pregnant wife. I was quickly becoming bored.

Although she had opted for natural childbirth, Stacey was handling her contractions with relative ease. We worked on her breathing and walked the halls to aid the process. All was doing well, until she wasn't. With little warning, her body was slammed with a severe contraction that made her catch her breath. By the time the she was able to compose herself, she was hit with another that seemed to cause her eyes to roll.

As the nurses rushed into the room to silence the machines and check on her, I slowly backed away to let them work. Something was wrong, and I was powerless to help. I heard the nurses talking: her last checkup showed she was only 4 cm, so the strength of her contractions was alarming. *What if she died?* I wondered. Would I be able to care for my daughter alone? I needed to be prepared for all possibilities.

Within minutes of scaling back her medicine, Stacey's contractions returned to a normal strength, duration, and frequency. It was the Pitocin, they realized—the drip was too strong and out-pacing the dilation process. Stacey looked exhausted.

"Maybe we shouldn't have turned down the epidural," she said ruefully. It was too late to turn back now. Our daughter was coming the old-fashioned way, barring any other complications.

As the hours wore on, Stacey got more and more frustrated with me. It was too hard for her to go through the pain with me watching her with so much concern on my face, she said. My show of support was actually hurting her efforts to deal effectively with everything that was happening. At the urging of everyone—including the nurses—I reluctantly agreed to leave the room. A dinner break would probably be best for everyone.

Leaving the hospital with her parents, we drove to a nearby restaurant for an early dinner. I didn't exactly like the idea of staying away, but with nothing to do, I accepted the guidance offered by those more knowledgeable. Although we didn't have the most intimate relationship, I allowed myself to enjoy the dinner and conversation with her parents. My thoughts were a thick haze and the distraction was a welcome escape from the anxiety threatening to overtake me.

When my cell phone rang, I knew my break was over. Answering my mother's call, she implored me to get back quickly. In the hour that had passed, Stacey had doubled in dilation and the baby had moved into position. If I didn't hurry, I was in real danger of missing my daughter's birth.

My years of reckless driving as a teen were the perfect training for my race back to the hospital. Any cop trying to pull me over would have had to talk to me at the hospital, because I was stopping for nothing. Arriving within minutes without incident,

I abandoned the car to my in-law's care as I ran to Stacey's room.

I arrived at the birthing room to see my mother soothing my wife and the doctor nowhere to be found. She had been notified but had yet to arrive. I took my place by my wife's side to support her through her pain and agony. Whatever anxiety I had was lost in that moment. Wiping the sweat from her brow, I comforted Stacey with the knowledge that it would be over soon. She was doing great work and in the midst of all things hectic, I told her how proud I was of her.

The doctor arrived and within seconds of taking her position, I saw the crown of my daughter's head. Another push by Stacey and her head was fully exposed, supported by the doctor's guiding hand. With one last forceful push, my daughter eased into the world.

Stacey burst into tears and grasped our daughter tightly as she was placed on her chest.

Despite all the hoopla, I was slightly underwhelmed. Although there was little crying on her part, her heart and lungs were deemed strong. With a piercing gaze, my daughter glanced around the room, taking in the sights and sounds, more interested than intimidated. Yasmine Marie Mwongozi had arrived.

Year 27: Measure of a Man

The first thing I did when we returned from our stay in the hospital was send my mother-in-law home. I needed space to enact my vision without her second guessing my every move.

My second order of business was to limit the amount of time Stacey spent tending to Yasmine in lieu of her own needs. I was very aware of the dangers of stress, lack of sleep, and the possibility of post-partum, and it was my responsibility to make sure Stacey got as much rest as possible. Luckily, I was able to take a few weeks of full paternity leave. I spent the time taking care of Yasmine while Stacey rested.

Once my leave expired, I made sure to resume my parental duties when I returned home each day. Aside from the times she was breastfeeding, I spent my time tending to Yasmine in every way: changing diapers—with the help of a large box of latex gloves—and soothing her whenever she was upset by getting on the floor with her or reading to her.

I made sure to speak to her in a manner that respected her as a thinking person, knowing that it would help her develop an exceptional vocabulary to match the incredible woman she would become. I wanted to instill in her the ability to master her thoughts and feelings and to influence and lead others. The Mwongozi home was in the business of raising adults, not children.

For all my plans and machinations, there was an outstanding issue that I couldn't resolve: a budget deeply in the red. The situation was readily apparent when we learned we were having a baby, but Yasmine's birth escalated the urgency. I studied our budget nearly every day trying to find a way to close the gap, but solutions evaded me. We had a pending $700 hole that couldn't be filled simply by reducing the utility bills or foregoing takeout.

Although Stacey worked for a childcare center, she received very little in the way of discounted services. The facility was contracted by a bio-tech firm and it was a breach of contract for them to discount the price of services for employees of the center. The only thing keeping us viable was a six-month grace period before full pricing ensued. From the day Stacey went back to work, we were on the clock.

Stacey's tentative idea of becoming a stay-at-home mom was met with a swift and stern dismissal. She'd always dreamed of starting a family and staying home with her children, just like her mother, but that wasn't an option. Though we would have saved on childcare, the loss of her income would have generated the same $700 deficit. And I'll admit I was also strongly opposed to the notion philosophically.

My only hope was to secure a promotion or new job by the summer of 2004, and it was to this task that I devoted every spare moment. I became a regular fixture on the job boards applying to any job that loosely fit my skill set and came with a promotion. Although there was some deference to the nature of the job, my main goal was a higher salary.

I secured a number of interviews, but the process wasn't moving as quickly as I'd liked. The passage of time was a direct measure of the increasing amount of pressure and stress I was under. Each passing day without a change in our circumstances increased my feelings of anxiety. Every moment spent with my daughter reinforced my resolve to do whatever it took to provide her the life I wasn't fortunate enough to have. In this matter, failure was not an option.

It was on an unremarkable day that my fortunes changed: I was called into my manager's office regarding a possible job offer. Ana was aware of my circumstances and was a greater advocate for me than I could have hoped for. She'd spoken to Annette, the hiring manager for a long-coveted promotion, but they had concerns about my commitment level for the job.

Although advertised as an opening in a number of cities, the location in need was an office in Tulsa, Oklahoma. Annette, being a Dallas resident, found it hard to imagine that a young California native would be willing to leave San Francisco for Tulsa.

"Tell her that Tulsa might be the greatest place on Earth, but I'll never know unless I go there," I replied without missing a beat.

Stacey turned out to be a tougher sell on the idea. Having no ties to Oklahoma, I needed to make a compelling case. It was a 4-hour drive from her parents in Kansas City, which was a strong incentive to overcome her resistance. The more we discussed our financial situation, the impact of the raise, as well as the additional benefit of a cost of living reduction, the more she warmed to the idea. It didn't take too long to realize that Tulsa was the answer to most, if not all, of our prayers. Once we finally made the decision, we wasted no time in leaving for our new home.

Tulsa was a non-descript town in a corner of a state I thought I'd never visit. Driving into town late on a Sunday morning only confirmed what I imagined the place to be. If you took a nap for more than twenty minutes while driving through it, you would miss the entire metro footprint. Big city biases aside, I was determined to make the best of use of my time. I wasn't there to have fun; I was there to provide for my family.

We checked into a hotel the first night and I noticed something curious but unsurprising: there were no black people. There was the one janitor, which I found to be ironic, but I hadn't seen any others. The city didn't feel hostile or unfriendly, unlike my first few weeks in Atlanta; it just had a lack of diversity.

Within a few days, we were in our apartment and unpacked. Already feeling a bit of cabin fever, I kissed my ladies goodbye and took a drive around town to get a feel for my new city. It wasn't much compared to the Bay Area, but the city had its charm. For what it lacked in scenic views, it more than made up for it with its beautiful neighborhoods, extensive parks, and low-lying hills and trees.

After driving for awhile, I stopped in a local bar. I wasn't looking for much; perhaps I could listen to some music before heading home. Walking into that bar, I was again reminded of my uniqueness relative to the patrons. It wasn't that I'd never been the only black person in a bar, it was just that those places were usually more upscale and in cities known for being more diverse.

I may have been in the bar for five minutes, when a gentleman sitting further down the bar called out to me. He greeted me, asked my name, and then offered his. He asked what had brought me to town, making it clear that everything about me screamed that I wasn't a local. My brief response concerning work was greeted with congratulations and the offer of a beer. Because I wasn't planning on staying long, I politely declined, but he made a point that it wasn't right to sit in a bar and not have a drink then ordered me a Bud Light on his tab.

We spent the next ten minutes talking about Tulsa, the state of Oklahoma, and listening to old rock tunes playing on the jukebox. I finished my beer and thanked him again. The man, with a name I couldn't remember, shook my hand and wished me luck in life. Driving away, I was taken aback by his casual hospitality but was certain that I was in the right place.

All in all, the move was revealing itself to be a great decision. There were growing pains, but the lack of financial stress was welcome. I don't think Tulsa was Stacey's idea of a long-term solution, but she did her best to accept it. And while she appreciated my work ethic, I found out quickly that she didn't exactly appreciate my devotion to my job.

After only a few weeks of being in Tulsa, I was called back to California for strike duty. I was determined to prove myself in my pursuit of a career within SBC, even if it meant upsetting Stacey. I was providing for my family, and that was what mattered most. As annoying as it was to be recalled, it was even more annoying trying to explain the importance of doing my job to Stacey.

"What am I supposed to do?" I challenged. "They called, and I have to go."

"But why does it have to be you?" she complained. "Don't they have someone else to do the job? What difference will *you* make?"

"I have no idea. I've been asking the same thing, but the answer is the same: I have to go back."

We decided it would be best if she spent the time with her parents in Kansas City instead of being alone in Tulsa with Yasmine. As my trip loomed, her disappointment with the situation continued to grow, even though she was happy to spend time with her parents.

"I still don't understand why it has to be you that goes."

This was becoming a common refrain. What started off as a discussion turned into a simmering argument that grew hotter with each iteration. She just couldn't understand why I had to go, no matter how many times I reassured her I'd explored all other options.

By the time I was ready to leave for my assignment, I was actually looking forward to a vacation from it all. I just wanted to be away from Stacey and her constant complaining. The morning before I was to leave, we stood in her parents' kitchen and she started in on me yet again.

"This just doesn't make sense to me. Why can't you do you the assignment here? Can't you trade with someone?"

"We've already talked about this. I have no choice; this is my job. What am I supposed to do?"

"You could quit," she offered.

"Quit?! Then what would I do?" I asked incredulously. Was she serious? I'd just taken this job. *This is starting to get ridiculous*, I thought.

"I'm sure my dad could get you a job at the Ford plant. They have good jobs up there."

"There's no way I'm working for your father. What does that look like? I went to school so I don't have to work in a factory. I'd lose a hand or something."

"You're being ridiculous," she countered. "You won't lose a hand."

"It doesn't matter. I'm not going to work in some factory for your father."

"You're acting like a bitch…" she murmured under her breath.

"What did you say to me?!"

Anger swelled in me.

"What did you say? Say it again!" I challenged.

"I didn't say anything," she retorted.

I know what I'd heard, but I had no way to prove it. I wanted to hear her say it again just to be sure, but she denied saying anything. *Did I not hear what I thought I'd heard,* I mused confusingly? My anger was off the charts, but we were in her parents' kitchen with them in the next room. I felt attacked, disrespected, and trapped—in the moment and in my new marriage.

She hadn't once tried to understand the situation or support me. She'd only attacked me the minute she found out I had to go back. *This isn't a person with your best interests in mind,* I whispered to myself. *She doesn't care about you; only her own wants. Don't trust her; you can only trust yourself.*

I shut down and didn't say much to her until it was time for me to leave. Even then, I barely spoke. I didn't call when the plane took off or when it landed. I was lost in my own thoughts of what had happened. I'd never been spoken to so disrespectfully by anyone I'd dated, and I wasn't going to accept it now just because I was married.

I arrived back in California and focused on the job I was sent to do. I avoided Stacey's calls for the next three days. I was so mad that I wanted nothing to do with her. I loved my daughter, and I would need a plan for her, but I was seriously contemplating leaving Stacey. This wasn't the type of relationship I wanted to be in and I wanted a way out.

I was so angry, I even thought about having an affair. I met a woman in a bar one evening during my assignment, and she seemed to be a convenient answer to my current feelings. My friends tried to warn me about compromising my morals, but my hurt feelings wanted comfort. I invited her to have dinner with me, ready to commit to the affair, but I lost my nerve sometime between the appetizers and dinner. This wasn't the man I wanted to be.

It was a week before I returned home. Somehow, we moved past the issue and focused on making a life for ourselves in Tulsa. I put my energy into my new position while Stacey researched schools for Yasmine and looked for work. We spent a lot of our free time together getting used to our new city, checking out neighborhoods, and looking for a home to buy. On the surface all seemed okay, but each day felt like a struggle to get through.

In many ways, we were still getting to know each other. The balance we were able to maintain was sufficient to get through life, but I couldn't say I was happy. There were aspects of life that were fun and joyous, but I couldn't shake the feeling that something was missing. I had a beautiful child and a good wife, but this wasn't what I'd imagined my life would be. The more I tried to be happy, the more I felt that hole. What was missing, I knew, was Dayna.

Most of my friends and family, including Stacey, thought I still mourned Dayna from a place of desire. This was a rather insulting perspective of what I missed. Dayna had always been my best friend and the one with the wisdom to see past our moments of struggle. She was the one person in the world that understood who I was, who I wanted to be, and had the best ideas for how I could get there. She gave me insight and confidence in myself; something I still hadn't mastered. I was missing that in my life and especially in my marriage.

The stress didn't help with my growing sense of anxiety and tension. Pressure-filled days were followed by restless nights. I had so much on my mind that I didn't even worry about a small rash that had appeared on my chest one Thursday morning. With the change in climate these things were bound to happen, I reasoned. By Friday, there seemed to be some mild irritation surrounding the area, but I still didn't take it seriously. Sunday morning when I awoke in pain, I realized something was really wrong.

I stubbornly spent a few more hours in pain before going to the hospital. I worried that it was the beginnings of a heart attack. The nurses at intake received my account of pain with a large dose of skepticism. There was simply no way that I could be having a heart attack, in their estimation. They dismissed my urgency, noting I was too young and not in any obvious distress. Besides, they told me, the cost associated with the tests were high.

"What do I care what it costs? I'm not paying for it; that's what insurance is for," I replied. I didn't even bother to hide my irritation.

Laying on a gurney with the EKG wires dangling off of me, I was at a loss for what might be happening. Despite how it appeared, I knew something was wrong and that I wasn't crazy. When the doctor appeared to check my charts, he wasn't so sure. He could see nothing abnormal, but he sensed that I wasn't making up my pain. Lifting my shirt to listen with his stethoscope, he noticed the rash on my chest and asked if I had noticed it as well. Acknowledging that I had but had no idea what it was, he seemed both shocked and relieved as he gave me his diagnosis. I had shingles.

From what I understood, shingles was something that only affected the elderly. While that was true, he cautioned, anyone that had had chicken pox was susceptible. As we discussed my life and health history, he determined that stress was the primary contributor to my condition. From his charts he could see that my blood pressure was elevated; the details of my life only confirmed his opinion of the matter.

"Young man, you need to find a way to manage yourself better. Stress is the primary cause for most ailments. This wasn't a heart attack this time, but you never know."

As a sharp pain coursed through my chest, I knew he was right. So much had happened over the past year; from the marriage and baby, to the new job and relocation, I was stretched thin and felt myself closing in on a breaking point. I needed to pull my shit together—sooner than later. My life was no longer my own; I had a little girl who needed me.

Year 28: Part 1 –
Make Yourself at Home

My desire to build a stable foundation for my family and a more tranquil existence for myself was strong. I remembered the pride I had when my mother bought our first home years before and the positive change it had brought to my life. Along with the sense of stability I wanted to give my family, I also wanted my daughter to have the room to play and grow in a place she could call her own. With these things in mind, we began the search for a home.

Despite being equal in desire for a home, Stacey and I were at odds over what our home should be. Growing up primarily in suburban areas, she wanted something similar to her upbringing. With so much construction in the Tulsa area, her dream of a brand-new home was well within reach. Why should she settle for a "used" house if she could have a new one, she reasoned?

I, on the other hand, wanted a home closer to the center of town. Growing up in cities, I liked the energy of urban centers and the easier commute into work. The affordability of Tulsa's market made my dream of a nice home in a nice centralized neighborhood accessible. My needs were modest, and I didn't want the large, useless spaces newer homes provided. In my opinion, older homes in established neighborhoods offered something the suburbs couldn't: character.

For the weeks we looked at homes, our relationship would undulate between supportive and contentious. For every home I liked, there were half a dozen issues she would find with it. She had no appetite for renovations which disqualified many homes. I liked many of the same ones she liked, complete with new appliances and modern kitchens, but I didn't like the locations or the sameness of the subdivisions. We were at an impasse with few options for a bridge solution.

On a drive through town one day, I found what I thought was the perfect resolution. Situated on a quiet street in midtown, the home I found was newly renovated with three large bedrooms, two bathrooms, and a large backyard. It seemed to be the perfect blend of what we both wanted, and I was excited to share my discovery with her.

During our walk through together, she was impressed with the find. It was a nice home in a nice neighborhood and only needed minor work. There was, however, one issue that was hard for her to deal with. The washer and dryer were not in the main house, but in the garage. While large enough to accommodate washing facilities, it was only large enough to fit one car. In her mind, the house was no longer acceptable.

I began to lose patience with her and her long list of wishes. For the neighborhood and the price, in my opinion, the house was a steal. And even though the location of the washer and dryer were in the garage, they were still acceptable. I was focused only on finding a suitable home while maintaining maximum financial flexibility, but her attitude about it was pushing me to my limits.

By nature, I was a net saver with a decent portion of my salary devoted to long term investments. Her attitude was to spend and enjoy her money in the moment because "tomorrow was not a certainty," she would say. I decided that as the sole provider of down payment funds, I would buy the house that *I* liked and fit into my financial philosophy. She wasn't happy with my decision, but ultimately decided to let the argument go.

After we settled into our new home, we turned our attention to our reason for being in Tulsa: Yasmine. After an extensive search, we settled on a child care facility at a downtown church. Among many things we liked, it was also across the street from my office allowing me easy drop-off and pickup. Stacey's new job was on the other side of town, and she was happy for one of us to be close to Yasmine at all times. We were encouraged when her new teacher, Cynthia, requested a home visit in anticipation of the new school year.

She was a pleasant woman and I found her to be kind and friendly during our meeting. The more we spoke, the more I liked her and felt comfortable with her taking care of my child during the day. While we were initially concerned about the level of care Yasmine would receive as Cynthia's own daughter would be in the same class, Cynthia was a professional and would not play favorites. Stacey, being an expert of early education, was also impressed with Cynthia and seemed at ease with giving this woman charge of our daughter while we worked. Knowing that Stacey approved made it that much more apparent that it was the right choice.

Over the course of the meeting we'd discussed our brief tenure in the area and that we hadn't made friends. In getting to know our family, she disclosed that she felt a strong connection to us and was sure that her husband and I would get along great.

I liked Dave immediately. At 6'9" he was the tallest person I'd ever met, but aside from his imposing size, he was a big kid. We became fast friends and bonded over our shared love of video games, music (he was a bass player), dark humor, being fathers of girls the same age, and a variety of other things I can't remember. I do remember, however, leaving their home thinking that the whole occasion was a pleasant surprise and much different than what I'd expected.

I wasn't sure what I expected it to be. At the age of twenty-seven, I didn't know any white people and didn't have white friends. I had no idea of who they were, how they lived, or what life was like for them. Aside from the few acquaintances I'd had in high school or at work, I didn't know them intimately. I wasn't racist by any stretch of the imagination; I just didn't have contact with white people in that way. After the social sorting that occurred in junior high school, having white friends just wasn't a thing. My only ideas of how white people lived were from television.

Aside from episodes of *Roseanne* and *All in the Family*, white people were portrayed to be pretty well off. Not everyone was rich, but they didn't seem to have to deal with the same issues I did. They were just different people, living different lives, in a country that seemed different than the one I lived in. As much as I thought I knew about white people from media and mainstream culture, I realized that I didn't know much at all.

Dave and Cynthia were regular people, with a regular family, living in a regular city. Making ends meet, with enough for the occasional vacation or luxury item, was a challenge we all struggled with. Their fears and concerns for their daughter, Elizabeth, were the same as my concerns for Yasmine. Aside from Stacey and I having better tans, we were essentially the same family dealing with the same problems.

I was falling in love with my new city. Above all, it was the people that I fell in love with. The feelings of warmth and hospitality I'd experienced at the beginning only deepened with time. Underneath their conservative Christian exteriors and social views, the people of Oklahoma were the most loving and caring people I'd ever met. It was second nature to invite someone over for a meal or to invite one to spend a Sunday morning at their church. The spirit of church and community greatly informed their behavior and attitudes towards the well-being of others; the only requirement was for your work ethic to be strong and your excuses few. Not everyone was conservative, but the culture of kindness was strong.

Unfortunately, the more I settled into life in Tulsa, the more unsettled my life with Stacey became. As I grew closer to new friends, she and I grew further apart. I couldn't figure out what the issue was, but it seemed to get worse every day. I loved my wife, but she seemed perpetually unhappy and I had no idea how to fix our relationship. In many ways, she felt she lived in Dayna's shadow no matter how many times I assured her that wasn't the case.

It would be disingenuous to say there wasn't a basic level of comparison; every situation or relationship is gauged against past experiences. Despite this natural fact, however, I didn't pine for Dayna in spite of Stacey. I missed Dayna and the connection we shared, but she was gone and no amount of desire could bring her back. Even if we shared a special relationship, we were not without our share of flaws and troubles. I couldn't get Stacey to understand this and eventually stopped trying.

Finding the receipt from my dinner in San Francisco was the last straw. Coupled with my cell phone records, she was able to piece together enough information to confront me. Even after challenging her to call the girl in San Francisco—which she did—and confirming that I hadn't slept with her, Stacey was still angry. The fact that she had searched for evidence of me cheating without cause was proof of her contribution to the mistrust and hurt feelings in our relationship, but she refused to see that.

From my perspective, it wasn't this one event but a series of events that brought us to that point. From our conflicts regarding her being a stay-at-home mom to my insistence that I wanted no more children, we were always at odds. On top of that, the home I'd purchased for us didn't match her vision of a life for us and felt like a prison. She said she wanted out, and there was little I could do to convince her to stay.

In all honesty, I was happy to see her go. Not a year ago, I'd wanted out myself, but I had tried to make it work. No amount of effort ever seemed to give her lasting happiness. I was tired of everything about her, especially her constant disappointment at not living the lifestyle she wanted and her insecurities about my past relationships. I'd worked too hard building myself back up to be with someone who didn't appreciate me.

For the next couple of months, we lived apart; frozen in a

stalemate of wills. As much as I wanted to move on with my life, I was constrained by two things: my love for my wife and daughter. No matter how angry I was with Stacey, I still loved her. I'd made a vow to love and protect her always and the thought of going back on my word turned my stomach. No matter how stubborn and difficult she could be, she was my wife and I loved her.

Yasmine was a different story. When I held her, or smelled her hair and neck, a powerful wave of emotion would overtake me. In my eyes, she was pure love and joy incarnate. Surely I could resolve my issues with her mother in order to provide her the stable, two-parent home she deserved. In order to save our relationship, we needed to let go of the past in exchange for a future together. We had to admit our failings as people in order to help each other grow.

It is with this change of heart that I approached my wife with a peace offering. There was nothing more important to me than the viability of my family. As a show of my commitment, I would sell my family home in California as well as the home in Tulsa in order to purchase a new home for us. This time, we would choose it together.

Year 28: Part 2 – Common Ground

I'd resisted selling the home in Oakland, but holding onto the past was keeping me from embracing the future. My relationship with Stacey still had a high probability of failure, but if it had any chance of working I had to be all-in. I refused to be the reason my marriage failed.

I didn't even protest when she decided that she needed a new car, even though it was the fourth one she'd had since I'd known her. She'd settled on a Volvo Jeep. My only stipulation was that we take advantage of the European pickup program. This would allow her to get the car she wanted, while also giving us the opportunity to take a nice vacation with each other. She agreed and we made plans to pick up the car. I was still driving the Mustang my mother bought for me when I was in college, so we decided her new car would be the family car.

One day shortly after, she called to let me know our plans had changed.

"I stopped by the Volvo dealer and they had the SUV I wanted on the lot."

We'd just spent the past few months discussing how hurtful it was for me to make a financial decision without her input, and she was doing the exact same thing. Moreover, we were losing the vacation that I thought we desperately needed to fully mend our relationship.

The first time we have an opportunity to do something as a team she shows you that she's only out for herself. This is her instinct, I thought. *You're only here to maximize her happiness.*

But what could I do? The deal was already made, and I couldn't exactly take the car back. *If you protest now, she'll just make you out to be the bad guy, always keeping her from her dreams.*

Over the next few weeks, I stewed over my feelings. I hated that she'd reneged on our agreement and the powerlessness it spawned in me. It was the same feeling I'd had when she'd gotten pregnant. Of course I played my part in making the pregnancy, but that was the end of my decision-making power. My life was forever changed and my reproductive rights were secondary to the whims of another. The more I thought about the course of my life and the lack of agency I felt, the more determined I was to take back control. I wanted a vasectomy.

"But I want more children!" Stacey exclaimed when I informed her of my decision.

"I don't," I said flatly.

"That's not fair! You can't make a decision like that without my input."

The irony of that statement hung in the air as I fought to suppress pointing it out.

"I grew up with siblings and it was special to me. And what about Yasmine? She'll miss out on having someone to grow up with and play with!"

"She'll make friends at school. We had to move across

country because we could barely afford one child. I'm not trying to add to that stress."

"You can't make that decision without me," she countered again.

"Think about it all you want," I laughed. "I'm not changing my mind."

I'm not sure how she figured she could get her way. I was making a decision about my body and her input wasn't required. Perhaps she thought there would be another accident and I would be forced to accept it like last time, but that was an easy thing to guard against. I would simply refuse sex until the vasectomy was complete.

In all honesty, my physical attraction for her was severely diminished by her weight gain. I understood a large part of it was due to the pregnancy, but there was no urgency to resume her past habits of diet and exercise. It may not have been politically correct, but it is how I felt. Plus, it was hard to feel sexy and amorous when there was a constant level of tension in the air.

Exercising my power over such a crucial aspect of our relationship provided a measure of relief. As her frustration with me grew, I felt a sense of pleasure and satisfaction. For nearly two years I had been at the mercy of her decisions, and it was my turn to wield unchallenged power. There was only one way for this situation to be resolved: complete surrender on her part.

Emboldened by my newly recognized power, I looked for additional ways to extract concessions from my wife. With so much of my life and finances being funneled to buying a house that met her approval, I decided to use my annual bonus for solo international vacations.

A few years prior, I'd overheard a Nigerian businessman discussing life with a Houstonian colleague of his. Among other things, he talked about the importance of taking sabbaticals away from business and family in order to recharge the spirit and mind. At the time, I was as perplexed as his colleague as to how that level of freedom was possible given the various responsibilities assumed as husbands and fathers. The Nigerian's response was that sabbaticals weren't in opposition to, but rather in support of everyone's emotional well-being.

A man must have the opportunity to heal himself.

"What about Yasmine's college fund? What if we need something for the house? It's not fair that you take that money for yourself."

"We were supposed to take a trip together, but you decided to buy a car. That's what *you* decided to do with *your* money, so this is what *I'm* deciding to do with *mine*."

As much fun as I was having at her expense, I knew I was being petty. *You should be taking every opportunity to build with your wife instead of looking for ways to tear her down*, I cautioned myself. *You don't have to win at her expense*.

Even though it would feel good to go alone, I realized that a yearly trip together could serve my need for adventure as well as strengthen my marriage. With a fresh perspective, I invited her to come with me. We could use the time away from our daily responsibilities and concerns to fall in love again and grow closer to each other.

"But what about Yasmine?"

"Your mother could watch her. Or I could call my mother; she'd be happy to spend time with her granddaughter."

"I don't know about all that. I don't even know how to swim."

"What does swimming have to do with anything?" I asked, puzzled.

"If we fly international, we'll have to fly over water. I don't feel comfortable about that. If we crash, Yasmine will be an orphan."

I didn't argue or complain about it; she had a right to choose not to go with me. I also had rights and was intent on using them. Although I was firm in my decision to take more liberties, I also understood that I couldn't be too aggressive if she wasn't getting what she wanted. We set about finding the perfect house to match her new car. This task, however, was more difficult than I imagined.

Many of the homes we viewed in Tulsa simply didn't fit our budget and desires. As with everything, spending more money always moved one closer to an ideal, but our budget could only expand so much. All the homes we viewed either required too much updating, had odd floor plans, or were one of many look-a-like homes in non-descript subdivisions. As were learned more about lots, home designs, and costs, we came to realize that the best way to get what we wanted was to create our own floor plan and hire a custom builder.

With our new plan, we dedicated ourselves to building our dream home. We researched floor plans, loan options, and spent many hours watching HGTV and their unending array of property programming. As we discussed different ideas and slowly formed a mutual goal, an old and familiar feeling returned to our marriage.

She was funny, smart, and the look on her face when she became excited was priceless and made me remember why I fell in love with her. We were a young, dynamic couple with a smart and beautiful daughter. The year had been stressful, but suddenly our future seemed bright and it felt like we were finally on the same page.

After six months of searching and planning, we were at last on stronger ground. We quickly settled on a builder, secured a lot, and finalized a plan. Our agreement to split the mortgage and house bills 50/50 would allow us to cover our family expenses, while giving us our individual freedoms to pursue our personal interests. Even with our own allowances, we agreed to let each other know when we were spending more than a few hundred dollars out of respect.

With everything finally in place, I was able to book my trip to Prague that spring. Although she'd declined my second offer to join me, she was sad to see me leave. It wasn't until I'd arrived in Prague, checked into my hostel, and was walking Charles Bridge that I realized how lonely my relationship truly was.

Standing on that ancient bridge, I looked across the river as the full moon shone down on me as if illuminating the fullness of my solitude. Although I was witnessing something far beyond the horizons of my youth, the moment was bittersweet. No matter the progress we'd made, Stacey and I were still far apart on so many fundamental things.

Year 29: Too Many Straws

I initially planned to visit Prague for a few days before heading to Budapest and lands further east, but those plans changed when I made a new friend outside of Prague's Jewish Quarter. Michelle, a nineteen-year-old undergrad looking for someplace to charge her iPod, sensed that I spoke English, and asked if I knew a place. I didn't know the area well enough, so I offered to let her charge it back at my hostel but was met with a suspicious glance. To put her at ease, I kept the conversation going and we spent the next few hours exploring the city. When she felt comfortable with me, we made our way to my hostel so she could charge her iPod.

After it was fully charged, we spent a few more hours together before I accompanied her back to her own hostel. She assured me it wasn't necessary, but the Tulsan sense of hospitality and generosity had firmly taken root, and I wanted to make sure she got home safe. By that point, we considered each other friends and made plans to visit each other again the following day.

We spent the next few days exploring and enjoying each other's company, culminating in an offer to visit with her grandparents in Germany. Although she'd grown up in

Monterey, her mother was a native-born German and had recently moved back to her childhood home.

"You're welcome to come along," she offered with a smile.

Although I'd planned on heading east, I couldn't pass up the opportunity to visit with a German family.

There was something timeless and nostalgic about sharing laughs and stories I could barely understand with people I hardly knew. Relatives and friends from the tiny village crowded the even smaller living room; filling it with happiness and laughter. From their mock indignation that my idea of good schnapps had gold flakes in it to their very successful attempt to get me drunk on the real thing, I immediately felt welcomed and loved.

"Du est hier willkommen and kanst jederzeit besuchen," her Oma said while hugging me tightly as we prepared to depart for Rome.

"She says you are always welcome here and can visit any time," Michelle translated.

The rest of my vacation was a blur. The endless array of piazzas, fountains, and monuments of Rome coupled with delicious gelatos, pastas, and pastries was akin to a fantasy.

Why can't this be my life? I wondered.

But there was no use in complaining about it. My life was set on a path and the only thing I could do was follow along. I loved my daughter and was okay with my wife. My growing distaste for it was irrelevant; it could always be worse.

The only recourse left to me was to return home and embrace what lay ahead for me. By this time, we were firmly into the building process and busied ourselves with creating our idea of the perfect suburban home. Watching the daily progress of our home was similar to the changes in my relationship with Stacey; it was growing more livable by the day, but it was draining my resources.

Just as I began to believe we'd found a balance, we were hit with unsettling news. Yasmine would not be able to enter first grade on schedule because of her mid-September birthday.

Knowing my daughter was already beyond her age developmentally, our only option was to enroll her in private school until second grade, at which time her birthday wouldn't be counted against her. I alternated between acceptance and anger about this, because one of the main reasons for having a house built in the Jenks suburb was to take advantage of better schools. Although the tuition would be manageable, it was another added expense we didn't need.

After months of research, we found an exceptional Montessori school for Yasmine. After another few months, we moved into our dream home. As I looked from the balcony of my master suite one morning, I couldn't help but feel a sense of relaxation and contentment.

Every room was easily larger than any room in the house I grew up in. There were enough bathrooms for each of us, and more rooms than we needed. There was even a room dedicated as a music studio and playroom for Yasmine.

You're a long way from East Oakland, I mused.

One evening, Stacey came to me, asking to talk.

"Yeah?"

"I've been thinking about your insistence to have a vasectomy and I'm okay with it."

"Really?" My interest was piqued. "What changed your mind?"

"Well...I've come to love our family the way it is. Just the three of us is perfect. As much as I want another child, I don't want to change what we have. And it would be easier to give Yasmine everything she could want or need if it were only her."

She's finally coming around, I thought as I hugged her. Too many fundamental things had occurred in such a haphazard way that this felt like a turning point. She seemed happier and I noticed she was getting back into old habits and shedding some of the baby weight. And it made me happy to see that she understood that I wanted the best for us.

After my vasectomy, our relationship grew warmer. Stacey seemed genuinely content, despite her maddening habit of constantly buying things for the house that I didn't think we needed. As long as she paid her half of the bills, however, there wasn't much I could complain about.

But the tranquil moment was shattered when I found out the position I'd moved thousands of miles for was being dissolved in the merger of SBC and AT&T. I had no idea what that meant for my continued employment.

I opted to work remotely until I could find out more, and although this relieved me of dealing with the stress of the office, it actually increased my overall discontentment. I spent the majority of the day in the home I feared we could no longer afford. Cooking breakfast every morning in our massive kitchen reminded me of the dining room that was never used, and my anger and fear increased.

Driving into town to transport Yasmine back and forth to school was only a proxy for how much money was being spent on gasoline and car maintenance. Although we were current on everything, the thought of losing my income and my ability to provide for my family haunted me and made me resentful of Stacey. I knew that it wasn't all her fault, but I couldn't control the rising sense of anxiety I felt.

Even the news that I was granted a position in the new company and allowed to work from home exclusively did little to quell the unease I felt. My dreams were haunted by the voice of Odis and others like him reminding me that my life wouldn't amount to much. It would take only one catastrophe to send my life spiraling out of control.

I was in desperate need of recharging and decided to take another trip to Europe. Although I'd spent the previous three months worried about our finances, I deserved a trip. *She gets to have the life she wants all year. It's only fair that I get to do something I want to do*, I rationalized.

This time, I would stick to my plan of seeing Budapest and heading further east. Aside from a general concern that I'd be staying in hostels, no thanks to the horror film that had recently came out, Stacey was exceptionally supportive. I think she realized how badly I needed these breaks.

The truth is I needed a break from her just as much as my daily life. She wasn't the wife I wanted, but she was the one I had. It's not that I didn't love her, but we seemed to live completely separate lives. My job was to provide as many things on her wish list as possible; my reward being the ability to take my solo trips. *It could have been worse*, I rationalized. *I could have had a baby with Kizzy.*

Almost as if I'd conjured her with my thoughts, I was surprised to see an email from Kizzy on the day of my trip. It had been years since we'd last spoken. I wasn't proud of how it had ended, and I saw her email as an opportunity to make amends.

Her letter was meandering, but the sentiment was fairly straightforward. She'd had her share of adventures over the years and had a daughter of her own now. She'd thought about our relationship and apologized for her behavior during our time together.

"I know that you loved me and I'm sorry I didn't appreciate it at the time."

I wrote her back, sharing her sentiments.

"We were young and I'm sorry for what happened to you. That's not who I am and that's not what you deserved."

It felt good to say sorry to someone. I was filled with so much resentment for so many things that this outlet was sorely needed. Thanking her for her email, I told her I was leaving town and would like to continue the conversation when I settled down in Budapest.

I arrived in Budapest on a cold, crisp morning and checked into my hostel, sending the requisite emails to Stacey to let her know I'd arrived safely. Seeing another email from Kizzy, I opened it to continue our conversation, but was surprised to find her tone as icy as the air in the city.

"I was just trying to be cool with you. I'm not trying to disrupt your family…"

The last I recalled, we were having a pleasant conversation and moving past the hurt we'd caused each other. This email seemed to be out of place with where we'd left it. Scanning my last messages sent, I couldn't find a reason for the shift.

"I meant what I said: I'm sorry for what happened. I never

accused you of disrupting my family. Was this message meant for someone else?"

Her return email was even angrier, accusing me of trying to play tricks on her. To illustrate her point, she forwarded my last email to her back to me. It was not the email I'd sent her.

With a nagging suspicion, I apologized again and wished her a happy life. It took me a few minutes and a brisk walk to find a nearby store that sold calling cards.

"Did you get into my email?" I asked Stacey after we'd exchanged our salutations.

"What?"

"Did you get into my email?" I asked again.

"No. Why would you ask me that?"

"Because I just had a conversation with someone and there were messages sent to her that I didn't send."

"I don't know what you're talking about," she denied. "Who were you talking to, anyway?"

We went back and forth like this for some time. Frustrated and running out of call time, I ended the call. I knew what she'd done and it incensed me. Not only had she invaded my privacy, she had the audacity to lie about it.

The old realization that this marriage wouldn't work resurfaced. It wasn't until I was somewhere between Budapest and Bucharest that I learned that all wasn't well at home. I read an email from Stacey, and she admitted she'd sent an email to Kizzy out of insecurity. She was having a harder time dealing with my travels than she had expected. It made me angry that she had done this, but I was even angrier that she was hiding her insecurities from me.

"I miss you so much," one email began. "I know we don't always see eye to eye and there are plenty of times that I want to knock you into next week, but somehow we make it work, day after day, week after week, month after month, and year after year. We've had a time or twenty where we thought we wouldn't make it, but all the crap we have been through has just made what we have so much stronger."

She went on to say that she knew that we wouldn't be happy together if she kept refusing to travel with me, and asked me to give her time to come around.

"I love you," she ended.

We exchanged emails over the next several hours and the depth of communication gave me hope that our relationship was salvageable; we only needed to communicate more honestly. It escaped me as to why it seemed so difficult to discuss our issues when I was home. More often than not, she would become so angry and hurt by the things I tried to say that I simply shutdown and wouldn't speak to her for days. This was not the way relationships were supposed to work, but perhaps we were learning to be better to each other.

By the time I'd reached Istanbul, however, I realized my optimism was misplaced. A full-blown crisis was emerging at home. Although her mother had come to stay with her while I was away, Stacey was falling into a deep depression.

"I have to come to my own conclusion that I will never be enough. No matter what I do to protect us, I will always have to live in the shadows of Dayna, Kizzy, and all the women you've dated...I can't do it anymore; it's making me sick—literally."

Reading her email was heartbreaking. It continued on like

this, touching on various topics but the central theme was consistent: she didn't feel loved and appreciated by me. No matter how much I'd tried, I couldn't get her to understand that it was her I loved. It was exhausting.

I spent the next couple of days discovering the city of Istanbul, trying to ignore the growing sense of dread I felt. Waking up early each morning, I set out into the streets to explore the untold number of allies and hidden places that made it unique. Climbing the ancient city walls, I greeted the sun rise everyday as if it were a long-lost friend. My afternoons were spent searching the bazaars and sipping sweet tea. Periodically, the call to prayer would sound throughout the city calling the faithful to worship.

At night I would sit alone in my hotel room, reflecting on all I'd seen. *This was the life I was meant to live.* No matter how much I tried, however, I couldn't shake the feeling of doom that threatened to consume me. As much as I tried to fight it, I knew where the problem truly lay: I wasn't really trying.

I'd bought the house she wanted and allowed her to create the look of a happy life, but I wasn't present to make it a home. I checked out so often that she might as well have been single. Our relationship had become transactional. I didn't know how to give more of myself to make any of it better, but one thing was clear: my wife needed me home. Without a second thought, I cancelled the last seven days of my trip and was on a return flight home within the next few hours.

I'd hoped to make a grand gesture by surprising her with my return. In mind my, I imagined it would be romantic to literally cross the world to be by my wife's side. What I didn't count on was being greeted with a fight.

"Where have you been?!" she yelled as soon as I walked through the door. "I've been trying to reach you for hours!"

"I was on the way home to be with you," I replied crestfallen.

She continued to berate me as I slowly withdrew into myself. I tried to accept it all as the product of her depression, but there was something deeply personal about the attacks that were leveled towards me. A large part of me wished I'd stayed in Europe.

I resented her. No matter what I did or said, it never seemed to be enough for her. Every gesture was greeted with suspicion; every explanation was thought to be a manipulation. While she was consumed with her own feelings of depression and inadequacy, I slipped into a depression of my own.

I knew without a doubt that I wanted out of my marriage in its current form. I wasn't sure if I wanted to be divorced from Stacey, but I knew I didn't want to be married to her in this fashion. This wasn't the way I wanted to live my life, but the idea of divorce scared me. Remembering my own father leaving filled me with more dread than I'd cared to think. The idea of putting Yasmine through that was something I couldn't abide.

I spent the remaining spring and summer of 2006 dedicated to fixing my marriage. I tried to recognize my own patterns in an attempt to correct them. I even tried to take on more financial responsibility to alleviate her stress. The downside of this dynamic is that as her stress diminished mine increased. The negative energy could never be contained because I had no real idea as to the source or an effective way to stop it.

Despite the increased financial load I'd assumed, Stacey was still unhappy about finances. Even though we'd adjusted the percentage of responsibilities, she still didn't have enough extra money for her liking. This didn't sit well with me as we had explicitly agreed on a 50/50 split when we purchased the house and I'd already given her a concession on that. It was difficult for me to understand how our last agreement was already obsolete just a few short months later.

"How can it still not be enough for you?"

"I don't have enough money to do what I want to do, but you take all of your money and go traveling. What kind of man spends thousands of dollars traveling and leaves his family?" she'd asked.

"You've always been welcome to come, but you choose not to. You wanted this house. You want new cars. That's how you spend your money; I spend mine on trips."

As the conversation grew more heated, I had enough of the blame and demanded to see her finances.

She hesitated, but I was insistent. Even though I believed couples should maintain a certain level of financial autonomy between themselves, an audit of her finances was warranted since she was requesting that I shoulder even more of the family's financial burdens. I intended only to help her manage her finances and justify a reason for me to give her more, but what I found obliterated any goodwill I may have had.

I knew she'd spent a large chunk decorating the house when we moved in, but that was justified. Her other expenses, however, were beyond comprehension—she would buy clothes for herself and Yasmine, for seasons and events to come, even those years away. They were never full price, but she had closets of clothes with tags still attached.

Throughout our marriage, Stacey had remained unhappy. No matter how understanding I tried to be, it never seemed to be enough. No matter how much I gave of myself, she never seemed to be satisfied. There was always something just outside of my reach that was the key to everything.

As her husband, I accepted this fact. In many ways, I felt responsible to do all that I could to make her dreams come true. I loved my wife and wanted her to be happy above any and everything. But as the years and months had accumulated, I'd slowly lost me will to fight.

"I can't do this anymore," I proclaimed.

My capacity to give had been exhausted knowing that the culmination of my efforts would never be enough for her. I was hurt, depressed, frustrated, and exhausted. In stunned silence, she watched me put on my jacket, grab my keys and leave.

With nowhere else to go, I drove to Dave and Cynthia's house. By this time, I was as close to them as I would have been to any natural family member. They knew the problems Stacey and I were having, and they were neutral parties that only wanted to see us happy. I was glad for them, because I had no other place to go.

I didn't want to leave Stacey—I loved her more than I had words to describe—but I was unsure of how to manage the pain and frustration that had poisoned my marriage. We'd spent months in family therapy and it had done little to help us find a way back to each other. I was at a loss. Cynthia, forever the best example of a good Christian woman, was sympathetic to my feelings but cautioned me against making rash decisions. Her message was one of forgiveness, understanding, and patience. The principles I was fighting for, as well as the example I wanted to be for my daughter, were greater than the pain of the moment.

I called my mother later that evening. Speaking from the same well of faith, her words were similar to those shared by Cynthia. She knew how much I loved Stacey and wanted to keep my family intact. Her words gave me the courage to call my wife and go home.

Over the next several weeks, Stacey and I attempted to settle a lot of our long-standing issues. She apologized, and insisted she loved me and cherished our life together. She'd put us in a bad financial situation and continuously blamed me for ruining her life, but I knew she wasn't all to blame. I'd made my fair share of mistakes and knew I was emotionally absent in our marriage, but I also knew we needed to move forward. I could see only one way to do that and maintain financial stability.

"We have to sell this house," I stated flatly.

"I know," she replied sullenly.

"I love this house", I continued. "You and I built this house. But as much as I love what we've built, it's too much house for us to live comfortably. I want to travel. I want you to have more spending money. Most of all, I don't want us fighting about money anymore. I want us to be comfortable for the rest of our lives and not living on the edge all the time."

"You're right. As much as I love this place, it's not worth losing our family over."

As summer turned to autumn and autumn became the holidays, Stacey and I found a moment of happiness. It would be the first—and possibly last—holiday season in our home. We both loved the holidays, and this one felt special.

I spent a lot of time working on myself in those months. I knew I had issues with patience, and I was doing my best to find a greater purpose for the raw energy I possessed. I'd made friends with a few local musicians and spent a lot of time attempting to produce various songs and projects with them. I also enrolled myself in German classes at the community college as an outlet for my constant need to learn and challenge myself.

Ever since my first visit to Germany, I'd felt a strong kinship to the country and culture. It helped that there was also a company, Hilti International, which maintained domestic headquarters in Tulsa where German-speaking skills were highly prized. I'd heard many great things about the company and was interested in seeking employment there. I hadn't had any projects at work for the last year, and was starting to wonder if my time there was coming to an end.

As I gained greater proficiency in German, I wanted to solidify my newfound knowledge with an immersive visit to Germany. As always, I was planning a spring visit to Europe and an opportunity to increase my marketable skill was an attractive addition. Instead of roaming through various countries, I would stay in one location in an attempt to learn as much as possible. Similar to the advice I'd given to Dayna, I planned to immerse myself in the culture of Berlin.

Stacey and I were still heavy into our house search and spent much of our time researching our options. Lately, I'd noticed a lot of homes being built but less being sold. In our subdivision alone, there were homes that were on the market for far longer than normal, and it was making me nervous. We enlisted

Cynthia's help and visited a number of subdivisions, reviewing new homes on the market.

The weekend before my trip, after a long day of home viewing, Stacey and I had some type of disagreement that marked the end of our outing. It was a fairly minor conflict that I didn't think much about aside from the tension on our ride home. When we arrived, Stacey and Cynthia stood at our kitchen island as Stacey thumbed through a real estate book. In an attempt to move past the tension and not waste the day being upset, I casually asked if she saw anything that looked promising.

"I see things for me and Yasmine."

Cynthia tensed up and I glanced at her. I could tell she was extremely uncomfortable. I was embarrassed and angry at the silent challenge that had been issued. The similarity to our fight in her parents' kitchen just a couple years earlier was appalling. To flippantly discuss leaving me in front of company stung in a way that was too sharp to ignore. I was insulted by how she conveniently forgot the tenuous ground we occupied and that I had only recently given her a second chance.

Instead of trying to discuss the problem, I shutdown. The anger I felt quickly melted away to indifference. I'd seen this scenario play out too many times to care. She would have her tantrum, sulk for a few days then question why I was being cold to her. The only thing that would help this time would be put 5000 miles between us as soon as possible.

A few days after our fight, I received a call from my erstwhile manager in New Jersey that my position was being downsized. I had sixty days to secure another position within the company or I would be let go. While I expected to receive this news, the shock of hearing it still hurt. Our precarious financial situation had just become worse and my worst fears were sixty days away.

Two days before I was scheduled to leave for Berlin, I received an offer to interview for a job in St. Louis. I could feel I was approaching a major nexus in the progression of my life, but I had no idea of the proper way forward. Should I retreat and go into crisis mode or should I continue pushing forward knowing that my current path was true? Surprisingly, the decision was easier to make than I thought: I would push forward and continue with my plans to go to Berlin.

Stacey was supportive of my Berlin trip but was apprehensive about St. Louis. She'd become comfortable in Tulsa, and the idea of uprooting our family and moving to a new city didn't sit well with her.

I understood her objection. We were firmly settled into the fabric of the city and it would be hard to leave our adopted families. In my mind, the upside to the new job was that it paid enough for me to keep a small apartment in St. Louis and come home for the weekend.

I saw this as a win. We could have the best of both worlds: the family could stay in Tulsa and I could stay consistently employed. But for Stacey, it was just another excuse to fight. She wanted me to quit and find another job. The revival of this narrative no longer made me angry; it only raised my level of anxiety and isolation. I wasn't sure what world she lived in, but my life didn't work that way. The financial pressures I was feeling were beginning to cause me physical pain and her cavalier attitude exacerbated it.

*****

For the next two days, the tension increased as my trip approached. I alternated between nausea and anxiety. I went into survival mode; my only thought was getting out of town as soon as possible. As we drove to the airport, Stacey was blissfully unaware of what I was feeling and the precarious state of our relationship.

"This is just what we do," she opined.

"This is not natural," I countered.

As I hugged my wife and walked into the terminal, I realized that things had to change.

Arriving in Berlin was a relief, but not a cure for what ailed me. I was tired from travel and exhausted from life. I met my host, wished her a safe trip abroad while I managed her flat for her, and promptly fell asleep.

I awoke a few hours later feeling slightly better, but still very anxious. The nap had done some good, but what ailed me would require something more substantial. Turning my phone back on to check my email, I was bombarded with a host of urgent messages—several from Cynthia. Stacey had needed an emergency appendectomy while I was in transit.

I called home to assess the situation. Cynthia brought me up to speed on what had transpired and assured me all was okay. The doctors were able to get to her in time to perform surgery and there were no complications at this point. Even knowing this, my anxiety was through the roof. I checked in with Stacey a few hours later and she assured me she was okay.

"Are you okay? What happened?"

"I'm fine; just resting. My stomach was sore, but I thought I'd eaten something bad. Before I knew it, I was in more pain than I'd thought possible."

She assured me everything would be fine with a few days' rest. I promised to check on her frequently and hung up the phone. Despite her condition, I had my own health issues to deal with.

The next day or so was spent trying to reverse the damage that my unhealthy stress levels were causing. More than jetlag, I didn't get any rest and couldn't get comfortable. I was also having trouble breathing. I knew I was having a series of anxiety attacks, but I was nearly powerless to get them under control. There were simply too many variables and I had no idea where to start.

I emailed Stacey to check on her and make sure all was well. She assured me things were fine and she was doing better. Back and forth via email, our conversation transitioned to the stability of our relationship, and quickly deteriorated from there. As I attempted to explain my concerns and frustrations, she seemed oblivious to what I was saying. Out of every possible answer she could give, she always chose the answer that maximized my level of discomfort and anxiety.

With each email exchanged, my anxiety continued to increase. I was feeling dizzy as I tried to convince her of the merits of my plan to stay employed and support the family. With a suddenness that frightened me to my core, my vision began to blur and the lightheadedness I was feeling threatened to become a blackout.

I could feel my heart pounding in my chest as each breath became more difficult to achieve. The more I attempted to fight against the tide pulling me under, the more it gained on me. It continued to consume me until finally I felt nothing—all of my feelings were stripped away, leaving a barren emotional plane in its wake.

All that remained was a singular thought: *I have to get out.*

"I don't think this is working out for either one of us. I'm done; I don't want to do this anymore," I emailed.

I received a reply almost immediately. "What does that mean?"

"I want a divorce."

Year 30: That's The Bad Guy

I knew it was wrong when I did it, but I didn't care. *No one is going to take care of you but you,* I reassured myself. I was shocked by the audacity of my deeds, but wasn't surprised. At this point, there should have been no surprises for anyone. The sickness within our relationship was evident to anyone who cared to pay attention.

For the next three weeks, I wandered the streets of Berlin with a noticeable lightness of spirit. It was as though I'd awaken from years of slumber and was seeing the world anew. Learning that I'd obtained the job in St. Louis was an added bonus. Colors were brighter and the sun felt warmer. I wandered the city, getting lost in the sights and sounds of a foreign place—and ultimately finding myself.

Like me, Berlin seemed to be wrestling with the same questions of past, present, and future. From the darkest of times, it sought to reestablish itself in a world that had forgotten it. Although the scars of the past were still visible, it wore them proudly as a symbol that a fertile future could be built from the ashes of destruction.

Returning home, I was perplexed at how upset she was. It was clear to me that we had reached an impasse and divorce was the best option; why couldn't she see it as well? For years, she'd told me I was ruining her life. She should have been happy.

When Stacey and I had first become a couple, I assumed that we would either work or not work. To me, if we worked, everything would be roses and champagne. If, however, this went sour, we could always hug, shake hands, and part on good terms. I thought this was not only doable but natural. After all, I'd witnessed my own parents maintaining a good relationship with each other and their subsequent spouses. Stacey had a different idea in mind for how things would end.

The last thing I wanted was for us to devolve into adversaries seeking mutual destruction. I wanted us to take time to collect our thoughts and figure out a way to settle things with Yasmine's best interests in mind while keeping the peace between us.

Stacey, on the other hand, wasn't content to let things settle.

"We need to talk about this, Roc."

"I don't want to talk about anything," I replied wearily. Talking things out never worked for us. I just wanted to relax and stop feeling so anxious all the time.

"You told me you wanted a divorce. I need to know what you're doing so that I can plan what I'm going to do."

"I'm not planning on doing anything! I just want to calm down before I decide on anything."

"Is there a chance that you don't want to get divorced?"

"I just told you I want to take time before I decide anything. If you force me to make a decision right now, you're not going to like what I have to say."

Although my primary reason for wanting the divorce was to

extract myself from a toxic situation, my secondary motivation was to relieve Stacey of that same toxicity. Despite how it appeared, I was still very much in love with her. She was still my wife and mother of my daughter and I felt a continued sense of responsibility for her and her well-being.

Most importantly, I wanted my daughter to grow up in a home of love, even if one home would become two. One of the few things Stacey and I agreed on was shielding our daughter from our issues. Throughout our marriage, we made sure never to raise our voices to each other in her presence. Even with a pending divorce, Yasmine's sense of well-being was our paramount concern, and we took great pains to make sure she felt safe at all times.

As a child who had come from a split home, I felt a great sense of shame for what I was causing. Growing up, I'd felt the effects of my parents split, even though it was mostly because of the lack of money. I didn't resent them for not staying together, but I know if they had, our financial situation would have been stronger. I wanted to do better for Yasmine.

Even if divorce was the right thing, I would miss living with my daughter on a daily basis. In so many ways, she was nearly an identical copy of me. I wanted to make sure I did an even better job raising her than my own parents had with me. I feared that I was already failing her, though. My only consolation was that I knew, with all my being, raising my daughter in a home without love was a far worse fate.

Although I would have preferred all of us to stay in our home as long as possible, Stacey was adamant that she had to get out. The space she needed in order to recover from her pain required more than our 3000-square-foot home had to offer. I tried to convince her to stay, if for no other reason than to maintain an eye on our long-term financial health, but she disagreed. We weren't friends and she intended to do all she could to protect herself and her child. In a few short weeks, she was gone.

Despite my insistence that I wasn't in a hurry and wasn't taking steps to initiate a divorce, Stacey hired a lawyer. In response, I hired a lawyer to protect my interests. No matter how much I insisted I wanted to work with her to find an equitable solution, she viewed me as her enemy. This was setting us on a dangerous path of animosity that would only benefit our lawyer's bottom line.

I began to research divorce and custody laws. I was determined to minimize the financial and emotional costs of a protracted fight while still focusing on what was best for Yasmine. I wanted to be sure that when our business concluded, we would still be a family.

No matter how much I tried, there was no way to make Stacey understand I had her and Yasmine's best interests at heart. She didn't believe me or my intentions. The realities of divorce were far more complicated than a caviler email sent in despair.

Year 31: Part 1 – Hustle & Flow

My divorce from Stacey was declared final a week after my thirty-first birthday. I had a new sense of freedom and felt more alive than I had in years. I had no idea what the future had in store, but I knew exactly what the past held and I wanted no more of it.

I'd liquidated most of my retirement to provide Stacey a settlement as well as settle my half of the family debt. What was left, however, was a mortgage that was strangling me. Stacey had an apartment to maintain for herself and Yasmine and had few resources to devote to our combined mortgage. Luckily, we'd managed to pay for Yasmine's entire school year upfront, but there wasn't much left over for anything else.

The beautiful home we'd built together was cold and lonely. I'd turned the furnace off to eliminate the risk of being saddled with a high bill. Fortunately, the house was well insulated and wearing a full sweat suit and a blanket was enough to maintain a sense of comfort.

Any extra money I had after all my bills were paid was reserved for food and gas. Leaning on the wisdom imparted to me in my youth, my diet consisted of beans, pasta and vegetables.

When I had Yasmine with me, I'd splurge on a whole chicken, but that was my only indulgence.

I didn't tell anyone what I was going through. I felt guilty and knew I deserved it. And while I had good friends who'd been supportive of me and Stacey during the divorce, I didn't feel comfortable sharing the details of my financial difficulties with people. Despite my attempts to hide it, my friend Mike seemed to realize what was going on.

Mike was the leader of the band that Dave and my other friends played in. Sextion 8 frequently played weekend jams around town and the occasional show in cities around the region. After my divorce, going to see the band was all the entertainment I could afford.

One night, shortly after my divorce was finalized, I was helping the band load up their gear after a show. We were all intending to go out and get something to eat. After all the gear was stowed, Mike pulled me to the side and put fifty dollars in my hand.

"I love you, brother. Anytime you want to help us load, I'll put a little somethin' somethin' in your pocket. If you ever need anything, just holler at me."

As I shook his hand and hugged him, I fought hard to hold back tears. Even though it wasn't a lot of money, fifty dollars was the difference between having nothing to eat and eating decently for a week.

As much as I appreciated the outpouring of love and support, I hated the reason for it. I hated being poor. I hated everything about poverty, from the food to the mind state and broken spirits. I lived in a beautiful house in one of the nicest neighborhoods, but I was just as poor as anyone living in the hood.

I needed a second job ASAP. I was in survival mode with my back to the wall. I just needed to hold out until my house sold.

Swallowing my pride, I made my way to the mall and looked for stores I'd be interested in working at. When I got to the center of the concourse, I noticed a table outside of the Express store. Seated at the table was Kurt—a guy I knew from the various musician and artist circles I frequented. I didn't know him well, but we were familiar enough for me to go talk to him. Within thirty minutes, he'd introduced me to his manager, I filled out an application, and was hired on the spot.

I was able to breathe again, and started thinking about the future. Although I loved Tulsa, I knew that my life would ultimately take me away from it. I wanted to find love and happiness again. I'd made so many mistakes by not pursuing my desires, and I wasn't going to allow that to happen again. With this in mind, I called Shaina. I was intent on not letting another moment pass by without telling her how I felt about her.

She knew how I felt about her, long before I did. She'd known for years, and was disappointed that I lacked the courage to be honest with her. She was right that I lacked courage, but there were other variables at play that I had no idea how to resolve. She had, after all, dated one of my best friends and I had dated her best friend. Although these were brief dalliances from our high school days, my sense of loyalty made them difficult to overlook. We laughed at my rigidity and promised to always be honest with each other from that point on.

Although I felt free to express my true feelings for her, I was concerned about the health of our overall relationship. She had been my friend for years, and I was apprehensive about losing our connection. I valued her more than I'd ever value the opportunity to be intimate with her. If we were to embark on this path, I wanted to protect what we had.

She shared my sentiments, and we agreed to always love and care for each other no matter where this path ended. Having alleviated myself of my precarious financial situation, I had the ability to travel to see her. Because of our schedules, we settled on a week in late December for me to visit her in New York.

Arriving in New York, I was excited to see Shaina. I hadn't seen her in nearly two years, but this time the circumstances were much different. We were merely friends before; the idea of becoming lovers both thrilled and terrified me. As much as I knew her and wanted her, a part of me was worried about the optics. I had been divorced for only a few months at this point. There were also a lot of similarities with this and my story arch with Dayna. I sincerely wanted this relationship to stand on its own merit.

For the first three days, our time together was something out of a dream. Having previously only spent a few hours in New York, I was amazed at the pace and scope of the city. Staying in Park Slope, the neighborhood feel of New York was a pleasant surprise. More importantly, Shaina and I were able to rekindle our old friendship with the added bonus of being free to express the true depths of our feelings. After so much heartache, my sense of optimism for the future was increasing.

It was on the third day, however, that everything changed. Early in my trip, Stacey had figured out where I was. She was angry that I hadn't informed her of my plans and was calling me frequently. I was able to ignore those calls for the most part, but the message I received that day required my immediate attention. After being on sale for months in a soft market, we finally had a strong buyer for the house. Negotiations had intensified rapidly between our respective brokers and they needed my guidance on how I wanted to proceed.

Shaina, understandably, was upset at this intrusion into our time. To be fair, she'd dealt with the incessant ringing of my phone for a couple days. I did my best to ignore them, at times turning my phone off. She understood that it wasn't my fault, but after a while it became irksome. In this situation, however, I had no choice but to take the call.

Our impasse was due to the financial implications of the call. For months, the mortgage of the house had been a millstone around my neck. I finally had some relief due to my second job, but there was no long-term option other than to sell the house. Failure to sell would eventually result in a bankruptcy filing; that would be a devastating turn of events. Contemplating a future with Shaina, it was imperative for me to protect my credit for the benefit of us both.

I was also bothered by her insensitivity towards the situation. At some point, money and financial issues reign supreme. It was easy for her to give advice about what I ought to do, because it wasn't her money. Her only concern was what felt good to her in the moment. I wouldn't say it made me angry towards her, but she had unknowingly aggravated an extremely sore spot in my psyche. As her work week became more stressful and I dealt with my financial issues, a schism began to form that was troubling to us both.

By the end of the week, we weren't on the best of terms. We weren't angry with each other, but we were concerned with the troubling variables swirling around us. Her time in New York wasn't going well and she was under a tremendous amount of stress. Her work and roommate/landlord situations were taking a toll, leaving little emotional space for anything else. When paired with all the things transpiring in my life, we were misfiring more than we were connecting.

After my return to Tulsa, we gave each other a few days to contemplate our time together and to figure out what we wanted. When we did speak, she was understandably distant, stating she needed space from me. I couldn't blame her for not wanting to pursue a romantic relationship, but I got the distinct impression that our friendship was in jeopardy. She assured me that we would still be friends but asked that I let her initiate our next contact. Knowing that our relationship would never be the same, I hung up the phone, heartbroken.

Year 31: Part 2 – Chasing

Although the buyer liked our home, the price was above their budget. On top of that, they also needed to find a buyer for the home they were selling. The most ideal scenario was for us to swap homes with additional financing on our end to cover the difference with our original mortgage holder.

Their house was ideally located in a nearby subdivision. Not only was it a safe neighborhood, but it also provided access to our preferred school district if we ever opted for public school. I preferred to relocate back to midtown Tulsa, but it had the potential to be a good home for Stacey and Yasmine. The trick was getting Stacey to agree to it. Luckily, she found it acceptable.

Once everything was finalized, I found a suitable apartment in midtown Tulsa and moved in. While I still had my share of personal issues, I was in control of my own destiny. Things were looking up. And in my newfound freedom, I was finally able to secure a more lucrative job at the company that I'd coveted for so long—Hilti International.

Quitting Express was routine and I thanked everyone for my time there. AT&T, however, was a more complex issue. Working from home had sustained me for nearly two years, but I was eager to progress in my career. I knew AT&T wasn't a place for growth, and I'd already sacrificed too much time. I fully intended to quit after my first day at Hilti, but as I drove home, I wondered what the hurry was. I was in between projects, so I had a lot of dead time to do as I pleased. There was no harm in staying on the payroll for another week or so. The extra income would help. Besides, I could always quit later.

I was able to keep the AT&T job for about three weeks before a project came my way. I fully intended to quit then and there, but when I looked at the project I realized that I could complete it with little effort. There wasn't a definitive due date on it, so I was free to work at my own pace.

Did I even need to quit? Reading through the human resource documents of each company, I found no specific rules against having a second job. The only thing I found concerned conflicts of interests and direct competition. Given that both companies were in different industries, I was in the clear.

My only mandate was to balance my time. As I began to redesign the various processes and systems that I managed at Hilti, this became easier. Instead of creating value and giving 100% of my increased productivity back to the companies, I kept it for myself. If they hired me to do work that they estimated to take forty hours per week, why should I do the work in twenty hours and ask for more work? They sure as hell weren't going to double my salary if they refilled those forty hours. In my mind I was no longer an employee, regardless of what my taxes said. I was a small business owner selling my product to two customers.

Life was good. I couldn't believe how different I felt from three months ago, let alone a year. With my finances back on track, I began to spend more time hanging out and exploring the social scene of Tulsa. Tulsa was a great place for families—less so for single men in their thirties. As much as I'd integrated myself into the community, I was not a native. The consequence of this was that my network was limited to the families and married men I'd known while married to Stacey. Most people I met were single and too young or in long-term relationships stretching back to their mid-twenties. Nevertheless, I frequented many of the hotspots around town for the fun of it.

One such place was Kampai Lounge. It was part of a network of trendy bars in the Brookside District where people my age hung out. There was always a happy hour or birthday party celebrating a friend of a friend within my budding network.

It was during one of these many events that I noticed a young waitress working her rounds. She had an attitude that alternated between amusement and mild annoyance, depending on the table. She was cute, but not in an overt or flashy way. She was like the girl you knew in high school that was super cool, but you didn't realize was a knock out until years later when she stopped wearing sweats all the time. I was hooked immediately.

As the evening progressed I struck up conversation with a guy that seemed to be on the same mission as I was. From what I recall, Nate and I both knew members of a party celebrating someone's upcoming move to Dallas. Neither of us knew the guest of honor and were content watching the room. But without much action happening, the waitress was easily the hottest girl around.

He immediately called dibs and I didn't argue about it. I was never really comfortable initiating conversation with random women anyway. Being a strict adherer to guy code, I was content to play wingman as he struck up conversation.

She introduced herself, but I forgot her name immediately. That's just the way my mind works. Besides, her name wasn't really important. As far as I needed to know, her name was "chick my buddy is talking to." As Nate collected her number, I congratulated him on a good score. He could have done a lot worse for himself.

I didn't see her again until three weeks later. It was my first time back in Kampai, but I remembered her as soon as I saw her. We caught eyes and she came to say hello. Already slightly flustered by her presence, I was thoroughly embarrassed that I couldn't recall her name.

Her feigned sense of offense was cute as I explained the Swiss cheese that was my mind. Besides, I reminded her, she was talking to my friend. She admitted that she'd spoken to him a few times, but nothing had come of it. She was much more interested in me, but said I acted as if I couldn't be bothered. Her name was Renee.

I called her within the week and made plans for lunch. It had been a number of years since I'd been on a real date, and I felt out of practice.

We were both a fan of sushi so I suggested a place in Brookside, but it was a part of the same restaurant company as Kampai. As an alternative, she suggested their sister location on the south side of town. Although I was fairly nervous before the date, I was exceptionally so when we met up.

Sharing an array of sushi dishes, we told our individual stories with care-free abandon. We were both California kids that found themselves in the strange and alluring land called Oklahoma. She was from a deeply religious family but had shunned it as soon as she was able to leave her parents' home. I also didn't care much for having a personal religion but understood people's need for it. The concurrent status of our pending divorces was also something we bonded over.

The more we talked, the more comfortable we became. Losing track of the conversation, I slowly became aware of the intoxicating effects of her presence. Within the ebbs and flow of conversation, we simply stared at each other. We couldn't explain it, but there was a familiarity to us that needed no further explanation. We were just content to be with each other.

Leaving the restaurant, we headed to Bed, Bath & Beyond so I could buy a shower curtain. Although not the most romantic of gestures—it felt real and natural. Everything about being with Renee felt right and I urgently wanted to be in that feeling as often as I could.

I knew it was a bad idea, but I couldn't help but want her. As much as we connected, I knew she wasn't mine to have. She was in the middle of a tumultuous divorce and my own wasn't even six months old. As much as I felt that we could be happy together, I was sensitive to the fact that she needed time to heal.

The more I was with her, the more intoxicated I became. She was a drug and I was addicted to how she made me feel. It had been years since I'd felt seen, heard, and understood this way.

She was in the midst of a depressive phase, but I still wanted to comfort her. However, the harder I tried, the further she pulled away. Although I didn't begrudge her the space and time that she needed, the end result was that I was experiencing heartbreak yet again. Our relationship had barely lasted a month.

I sat with the pain of Renee for about a week before I realized I needed help. I wasn't worried about harming myself or others, but I had a very real fear of numbing myself to the rest of the world again. I'd hurt too many people to go down that path again. Having only recently awakened my feelings and sense of self, I was in no hurry to be buried again.

Pride and ego told me I didn't need anyone but myself. Slipping into a state of reclusiveness, I realized I was losing the battle of my internal struggle and could no longer afford to wait. I was a love addict and I lacked the perspective to keep my head above water. This was not an admission that my past loves were false; on the contrary, they were very real and meaningful.

The question I wrestled with was if I was worthy of being loved at all.

It was in therapy that I confronted this question that had haunted me my entire life. From the very first memory of my father leaving, I'd wondered why he didn't love me enough to stay. I know that my father loved me, but the seed of doubt had been planted the minute he'd left us. And every relationship after that had suffered. I'd always felt like an oddity, no matter who I was with—black or white, young or old, rich or poor, I felt like the opposite of everyone in my life.

It wasn't until Dayna loved me that I felt loved and accepted. It was her passion for me and understanding of me that helped me realize I was of value. No matter how much I'd fought against it, she loved me until I loved myself. And when I finally began to accept that truth, she was taken from me.

In the aftermath, my calloused pursuit of validation had hurt many people. I'd loved Stacey haphazardly and intermittently, only attempting to love her fully after I'd already sown the seeds of our destruction. Renee, Melanie, Kizzy, Shaina, and every other woman I'd been with had been a victim of my oppressive tendencies. I was an emotional vampire using the love and passion of others to feel alive and wanted.

Over the course of my therapy, I was able to finally admit this. Through the purging of my pain, I began to understand the responsibility of my birthright—being Rahmaan Mwongozi: The Most Compassionate Leader.

And then there was Yasmine. She was the gift and challenge I'd always craved. She loved me fiercely, but that love came with a high price. At all times, I was required to be my best self. I could no longer afford to think of my own selfish desires. My thoughts and actions had to be aligned with the best example I wished to demonstrate for her.

"Daddy, can we play?" she would ask after long days at work.

"Baby girl, daddy's tired. Can you give me fifteen minutes to rest? I promise we can play then."

She was strict when it came to collecting on such promises. There was never extra time given; she was insistent on holding me accountable. She taught me that I had to learn to laugh again and accept happiness when it arrived, not when I ordered it.

Most importantly, she taught me that the truest way to find the love I wanted in the world was to fill the world with the love I wished to see.

Year 31: Part 3 - Recalibration

As hokey as I may have previously thought it was, the power of affirmation was very real. Hearing my doctor tell me I was okay was the affirmation I needed. The sense of relief and absolution was tangible as a dark cloud lift from my spirit. She even offered to set me up on a date with the daughter of a friend. Although I turned her down, it was a testament to just how far I'd come.

I had a better understanding of myself, my inner pathologies, and I was determined to make better decisions in my relationships. Aside from my quixotic quest for love, I knew I needed to address my lack of career motivation.

When I'd started at Enron I had mapped out a plan to complete their three-year program, return to graduate school, and earn my MBA by the time I turned twenty-seven. From there, I would be in line for a 6-figure job, complete with an office and my own assistant. Growing up in the 80s, it was drilled into our heads that this was the ideal path to success. While the optics of success was in flux, the drive behind it was not.

After Dayna, a part of me had quit on myself. I found it difficult to sustain the requisite level of motivation required for achievement. When that was coupled with a difficult relationship with Stacey and the responsibilities of fatherhood, it was no wonder that my career—and desire for more—had stalled. The destruction caused by my divorce had necessitated innovative thinking but now with my reawakened motivation, I needed more. I decided to go back to school.

I knew it was a crazy idea, working two jobs and going to school, but that was the appeal for me. Most of my life, I'd created situations and manipulated people just to see what would happen. It was time now to turn that same critical eye onto myself in order to become a better man.

My pursuit to better myself led to a renewed interest in spirituality and religious expression. For years I'd avoided all religions, but I discovered a call to be around the faithful. I wasn't searching for a spiritual home; I was seeking insight into the nature of humbleness and service in the pursuit of ideals greater than one's self.

Tulsa was overwhelmingly a Christian community, but there was a diverse cross-section of other faiths I was able to explore. Some Sundays would find me visiting with Dave and Cynthia at their church, while others were spent in the local Catholic Church.

I visited Evangelical services as well as Pentecostal churches to experience Christianity through the eyes of new friends. I visited a synagogue for the first time as well as reacquainting myself with Islam through the local mosque.

What I learned was we as humans are all flawed and part of a larger community seeking our better selves through service, community, and grace towards others. Some times we're more successful than other times, but the real value was the endeavor of trying.

And so, with a renewed focus, I embarked on the journey of my own betterment. I settled into my educational and career goals, determined to make up for lost time. I was so focused and hungry for growth that I opted to forego the dating scene. My social energy was instead redirected towards my daughter and the friends that surrounded me. Besides, with my aspirations to ultimately leave Tulsa, I didn't expect the girl for me to live in Oklahoma.

I spent my time enjoying and celebrating my new sense of purpose. Months away from my thirty-second birthday, I felt young and powerful and wanted to enjoy one last beautiful Tulsan summer.

For months Kurt had told me about a wine and lounge music party that friends of his hosted. He talked it up so much that I was eager to see it for myself. Despite high hopes, the event was disappointing. Not only was the party sparsely attended, but the few girls that bothered to show up were women I wasn't attracted to. It was a dull party full of dull people. Even Kurt agreed.

I'm not here to meet anyone, I reminded myself. I was focused on my own growth and future plans, but I also understood it was important to connect with people. In this vain, I donned the character of loyal wingman to a guy I'd struck up a conversation with.

As wingman assignments go, I wasn't unhappy with my responsibilities. He chatted with the girl he'd been flirting with, and I chatted with the cute blonde who'd accompanied her. Jennifer was also not my type. She was pretty and blonde and I was sure she wasn't interested in me. Although I'd had brief affairs with Melanie and Renee, I didn't know a thing about white women and their dating habits. Her perceived lack of interest in a black man didn't bother me. As far as I was concerned, my only goals were to start and finish school—and secure a transfer out of the country. I wasn't looking for a relationship.

I continued making small talk with her and we eventually found ourselves sitting on a bench outside enjoying the warm summer evening. I'd intended to give the guy more alone time with her friend, but the more we talked the more interested I became. She was an accountant, owned her own home, and drove a Mercedes. She was cute and bubbly, but had a fierceness about her. I'd never met a girl quite like her. Her love of dancing and music added to her appeal—she was the full package.

Eventually, we made our way back to her friend and the guy I'd been wingman for. They wanted to continue the evening elsewhere. The only problem was both girls were drunk and Jennifer had been a passenger in her friend's car.

"How am I supposed to get home?" Jennifer asked, annoyed.

"He can drive you home," her friend said, pointing to me.

"But I don't *know* him."

"I'm standing right here", I replied. As interested as I had been a few minutes before, I was slightly irritated. It was getting late, I was tired, and I wanted to go home.

"You don't live too far from me and it's not an issue to take you home. I'm tired and want to go home. If you need my help, I'll help you get home safe."

Jennifer paused and gave me a hard stare as if she were attempting to read my mind. "Okay," she acquiesced.

It was probably my casual indifference that convinced her I

was a safe option. I honestly didn't care what she decided, but her accepting my offer made me happy. She was a sweet girl and I would have hated to leave her with less appealing options. As we drove to her house, she voiced her displeasure at the turn of events but was glad for the ride.

The ride to her house was pleasant enough. I got out and walked her to her door to make sure she got in safe. Realizing it might sound like a well-worn excuse to see a girl's place, I sheepishly asked if I could use her bathroom.

"I promise my only intent is to use the bathroom and leave," I said.

"Okay," she said, sensing this was true.

I was definitely attracted to her, but I really just wanted to use her bathroom, go home, and get a good night's rest. I had no desire to extend the night any longer or make a move on her. When she opened the door and two small dogs greeted us, I was even more determined to spend as little time as possible there. I didn't dislike dogs, but I was in no mood for them.

I think she was surprised when I exited her bathroom and walked straight to the front door. I wasn't drunk, but I was dead tired. The three-mile ride home seemed like 300 miles. I hugged her goodbye and turned to leave.

"Don't you want my number?" she asked, almost defiantly.

"Uh, yeah sure," I said, typing her number into my phone. I hugged her again before walking to my car.

Year 32: Part 1 - Unexpected

I spent the next week or so focused on work, enjoying the Tulsan summer. I was still managing my dual professions with a fair amount of ease, but I had identified a way to cut my workload in half. At times it felt like cheating — not because of infidelity towards either company, but because I'd found a cheat code for my career.

I was feeling good by the time the weekend arrived. It was the weekend of D-Fest, a growing musical festival in downtown Tulsa. As bands from near and far entered the city with their accompanying entourages and fan base, the atmosphere of the city changed. I made my way to the festival, excited to attend.

I ran into my old Kampai buddy, Nate, and we walked around, taking in the sights. When both of us were hungry, we made a plan to head to Brookside before the main acts hit the stage. He'd met some guys in a band from Denver and was eager to play tour guide around the city. With a few hours to kill before their set, we made our way out of downtown.

We all arrived in Brookside and parked in front of the restaurant, waiting for our group to reassemble. The Denver guys were cool, and everyone was in a good mood as Nate gave a brief explanation of the district. As we glanced around the area, we saw two girls crossing the street; one girl in particular captured our attention.

She wore a pair of shorts with three inch heels; her blonde hair flowing in the breeze. Her legs looked like they were cast out of pure bronze as they gleamed in the afternoon sun. We must have looked like cartoon wolves salivating over a pretty girl as she passed by.

"Hold on fellas! I know her…" I said as I sprinted across the street to catch up with her. Jennifer paused for a second before it dawned on her who I was.

"I thought you were going to call me."

I had no response. I hadn't called for a variety of reasons: I was working on myself; I was focused on my career and getting into school; I was planning on leaving Tulsa. None of these seemed like a good idea to mention, so I just laughed nervously and promised to call her during the week.

Early in the week, I sent a text. As she was an accountant, I knew her days were busy, so I kept our conversations brief. We texted off and on for several weeks, but I kept our conversations light. I asked her out several times over those few weeks, but each time she said was busy.

I didn't take it personally, but I was starting to think she wasn't as interested as I was led to believe. I liked talking with her, but I made a decision not to ask her out again. She was clearly very busy, and I had my own plans to attend to. It was probably time to let it go.

"When are you going to ask me out?" she challenged one day.

"I've asked you out twice already and you blew me off both times."

"Seriously? You asked me out last minute each time and I was busy. Do you think I'm sitting around waiting for someone to ask me out? I have things to do. If you want to see me, you ask me out properly and give a girl a few days' notice."

Damn…she was right. I smiled to myself, thinking, *this chick has a high opinion of herself.* She was borderline cocky about it too. Something about the matter-of-fact way she put it was sexy to me. She was no pushover and I respected that. I needed to step my game up.

I called her back on a Monday and asked her out for the following Friday. This time, she agreed. I didn't want to be too over the top, so I figured dinner and a movie were appropriate. There was a restaurant, The Celebrity, which was supposed to have an awesome Caesar salad. I intended to follow this by taking her to see the new comedy, *Pineapple Express.*

I hated first dates. Most of my dating life had centered on relationships, so first dates were always stressful events. This one was no different. As we placed our orders and waited for our salads, I found myself working very hard to keep the conversation alive. She wasn't rude or standoffish, but I couldn't figure out if she was shy or bored. By the end the end of dinner, her answers to my questions became slightly more expansive, but at best, I assumed the date was stuck in neutral.

By the time we made it to the movie, it seemed to be going in reverse. Admittedly, *Pineapple Express* wasn't a masterpiece, but I found it funny. Jennifer, however, looked like she wanted to be anywhere else.

When the movie was over, I was ready to call an end to the date. Deciding to give her an out without any confrontation, I extended an invitation to grab a drink or end the date. Unexpectedly, she opted to head to a nearby bar. Not sure what to make of the turn of events, I rolled with it.

We found a dive bar and ordered drinks. They were having some type of special on mini pitchers, but Jennifer opted for a standard pint. I followed the suit, assuming we would have a drink before ending the date. As we nursed our beers, however, our conversation seemed to flow better. Our bad date was getting better.

The waitress came around and we ordered a second round. By the time we finished our second beer, things were definitely more enjoyable. My attempts at humor seemed to be working and she seemed far more relaxed.

By the time the waitress offered us a third round, we were having a good time—good enough that when she ordered a third round, I felt comfortable giving her a little shit about it. By my count, we could have bought the pitchers and had the same amount of beer for half the price. Her reply was that she was a lady and ladies didn't drink out of pitchers on dates. I was really starting to enjoy her spunk.

I was surprised that it was ending on such a great note considering how the date had started. The next night, we talked and things were still going well. We both asked what the other was doing. I had no plans, while she was out with her friend again. They were going to a downtown bar and if I wasn't busy, I was welcome to join them, she said.

As I pulled up to the bar that night, my excitement to see her was immediately dampened by the sight of a car that looked eerily similar to Stacey's car. While Stacey and I had found the ability to parent together, she hadn't forgiven me for divorcing her. Any time our interaction exceeded sharing basic information about Yasmine, there was a high likelihood that the discussion would devolve into a re-litigation of our failed relationship. Hoping it was just coincidence, I parked and walked in.

It was when I walked in that I realized the situation was much worse than I could have imagined. A musician friend happened to be playing in the band performing that night and just finished their set.

"Hey man, did you see Stacey in here earlier?" I asked my friend.

"Yeah, she was hanging out with some girls. Are you guys meeting up?"

"Nah dude, I'm supposed to meet this new girl I've been seeing."

To make matters worse, a group of coworkers and their spouses happened to be sitting at a table in the corner. One of the wives noticed me and waved me over. Not wanting to be rude, I walked over to say hi, running into Jennifer as I made my way to the table.

I greeted Jennifer warmly and extended salutations to my coworkers. I gave everyone a cursory introduction. I didn't want to mix business with my personal life—and I was already in a near panic that Stacey would notice me. I quickly excused myself and headed to the bathroom to figure out a better plan. I returned to the group and pulled Jennifer away to explain the situation.

No matter what—all of my options were bad. It was best to just leave. The very last thing I wanted was to run into my ex-wife while on a date, especially with my coworkers there to witness.

"Listen, I'm told my ex is here and I think I should leave. It's a whole thing that I will explain to you later, but I should go."

"Oh, okay. I understand. Do what you have to do."

"I'll explain later."

By some small miracle, I made it outside and to my car unseen. I drove a few blocks, pulled over, and sent Jennifer a quick text to apologize again for my hasty exit and thank her for understanding.

In my absence, however, a coworker's wife had taken it upon herself to give Jennifer her opinion about the situation. In her estimation, it was obvious I still had feelings for my ex and Jennifer would do well by avoiding me. Jennifer, assuming this woman knew me better than she actually did, took heed of the warning and was upset with me.

"Hey...I want to apologize for running out like that. My ex and I don't really get along and I didn't want to have that type of interaction while you and I were on a date."

"But why did you have to leave?"

"Because I didn't think that was a good way to get to know you better."

"Are you guys not over?"

"Of course we are, but she's still angry with me."

"I still don't get it. What are you afraid of? Are you not over her?"

Regardless of how I explained it, Jennifer seemed to get more and more agitated. I understood her perspective but didn't feel that she was giving my perspective any credence. The more we talked the worse the situation felt; quickly reaching the point to where it seemed best to end things.

"Look…I did what I thought was best. There was potential for the situation to become nasty and I didn't think it was fair to put you in the middle of that. I was trying to be considerate of you. Maybe it was the wrong choice, but I did it for you. If that's not good enough, then fine, but I'm not going to feel bad for trying to do the right thing. I guess this isn't meant to be and I'm sad about that because I really like you. Take care."

Turning my phone off, I went to bed eager to end a terrible day.

I was still put off about the events of the previous night when I woke up the next morning and turned my phone back on. Shortly after, it started to ring. It was Jennifer. Not wanting to continue the drama but not feeling inclined to hide, I answered the phone.

"Hello?"

"I just wanted to call about last night. I thought about it and sobered up a bit and realized what you were trying to do. You were just trying to be discreet. I wasn't even upset about it until your co-worker's wife started telling me you weren't over your ex."

"I met that chick last week. She doesn't know me or my life."

"I get that, and I want to say I'm sorry about how I acted."

I couldn't begin to tell you the last time a woman had proactively acknowledged her mistake, let alone apologized for it. At a fundamental level, and after all of my failed relationships, it only reinforced my notion that Jennifer was a girl I needed to know.

Year 32: Part 2 –
Closer to My Dreams

Our relationship began slowly. No matter how much I tried, I couldn't quite figure out if she actually liked me. Like our first date, there was always a distant and awkward phase before things mellowed out and we ended having a fantastic time.

In the beginning, I spent an inordinate amount of time trying to figure out her feelings, but I kept calling on her, because the more time we spent with each other, the better it got. I seemed to be making progress, but I had no idea how or why. She wasn't excessively talkative or expressive with her feelings, but her actions told another story. Eventually, I resolved to just accept what she was offering at face value and not try so hard to figure her out.

It was when I stopped trying to figure her out that she began to make more sense: she didn't need me for anything. She wasn't impressed by my accomplishments and didn't care about my future goals. She cared in a general sense, but it wasn't awe-inspiring to her. All she cared about was that I treated her well.

And most importantly, she accepted me for who I was—

something I'd been searching for since Dayna. Despite never wanting to date a man with children, Jennifer accepted that I had a daughter. She wasn't concerned about my divorce; it wasn't her business. She was amused by my little idiosyncrasies, like getting cold quickly and not wanting my food to touch. There were no assumptions on either of our parts; we just accepted each other.

Being with her was something new for me. I'd never dated a white girl before—not for this length of time—and it took a while to reconcile my thoughts about it. I'd had brief love affairs with one or two, but I was never in a situation where we dated openly and exclusively. Within the year, we began living together.

Jennifer and I learned a lot about each other because of our ethnicities. As silly as it was, I didn't realize that all white people didn't have straight hair. Some do, of course, but many don't. Looking in her bathroom, I was shocked to discover she had just as many hair products as any black woman I'd ever known. I also learned more about tanning than I thought I ever needed to know.

I realized that so much of what we expect our partners to be is only partially attributed to our individual ideals. Most of what we think we want or desire is based on our culture, sub-culture, family, friends, and our idea of what is expected of us—even more so when you factor in religion, race, and ethnicity.

As I got to know Jennifer and grew closer to her, I wondered why her race registered to me at all. Being true to my ideals about people would mean that her race was not relevant. The more I contemplated the social and cultural ramifications of dating her, the less I cared about them. They weren't designed with me in mind at all. Those things weren't supportive of my individual ideals and were, in fact, counterproductive to my pursuit of happiness.

All I cared about was if a person was good to me, and Jennifer was very good to me. This isn't to say that there weren't things that we learned about each other due to our ethnicities; we were just willing to learn them.

Slowly and deliberately, we created a conceptual framework for our relationship. First and foremost, we were friends. Without an unquestioned foundation of trust, we understood that a relationship would not be sustainable. Our relationship was built on practicality.

We also created rules of engagement for arguments. We were both adamant that words have weight and consequences. You couldn't just say whatever hurtful thing was on your mind and not expect it to erode the bonds of the relationship. For me, this also included cursing and yelling. The point of any discussion or argument was to resolve the underlying issue, not throw water on a grease fire. And when an issue was settled, it was to be left in the past.

This was all very technical and admittedly unromantic, but we both had been in our share of bad relationships and were determined *to be better and have better*. We appreciated and respected the other's analytical mind and what it brought to our dynamic. The love we cultivated was an extension of the friendship we created.

Another thing that sustained us was our development and preservation of ritual. No fans of blind adherence to culture, we did appreciate the bonds and sense of purpose that culture could provide. Visiting family was important to her and she chided me for not making more of an effort to see my mother. With family scattered across the country, seeing our mothers was deemed non-negotiable, and we made yearly trips to visit them.

Of course, we still had disagreements, but we made a point to always respect the institution of *us* above and beyond our immediate feelings. We were both stubborn and proud at times, which could lead to very heated discussions, but we always found a way to come back to center. A great tool in our arsenal was food. It was sometimes comical for us to be in the middle of an argument and one of us calls a timeout for dinner.

There was one weekend when we pushing against all the safe guards we'd put in place. I have no idea what we were upset about, but it started on a Friday and lasted through Sunday morning. We had been together for well over a year at this point. It was one of those nasty fights where you hate to even look at your mate. I'm not sure we'd reach the point of breaking up, but our disdain for each other was palpable.

By Sunday morning, we were a couple days into our stalemate. Because Sunday brunch was one of our institutions, we were faced with the dilemma of being in public while holding onto our anger. I don't remember who made the call, but we challenged each other to get dressed and show up for brunch. Neither of us seriously considered not showing up—it was fundamentally ingrained in us that our absence was not an option.

We barely spoke as we dressed and made our way to brunch. We didn't even go to our normal place; choosing some place neutral instead. After we were seated and had ordered, we sat with each other in silence, neither of us willing or able to bridge the divide. And if it wasn't already awkward, Renee and her new boyfriend happened to show up.

We hadn't seen each other since we'd ended things. There were no bad feelings between us, and I felt comfortable enough to introduce her to Jennifer, but Jennifer was far from pleased. She knew who Renee was. She had no animosity towards her, but the very last thing she wanted at that moment was to meet one of my old flames.

We finished our brunch and headed home without saying much to each other. At some point during the day there was an unspoken agreement to let the issue go. I loved her more on that day than any other. She'd stood by my side as my partner and friend, even in the midst of our fight. I knew I'd reached a pinnacle in my ability to have healthy relationships.

Of course, there were the inevitable adjustments that came with living with someone, no matter how well intentioned we were. Despite the growth I'd experienced, I had moments where I wasn't my best. One of my biggest issues was money. It was still a sore spot for me after having been burned over finances with Stacey. I was very reluctant to allow Jennifer to give her input into my financial decisions, even though I always listened to her advice and perspective.

We also clashed over my relationship with Stacey. I harbored a lot of guilt over how things devolved during my divorce, and I sometimes made decisions from a place of guilt.

"Why do you give in to her all the time? Visitation, private school, all that stuff? You need to be more forceful with her. She's not your friend."

"I mean...sometimes it's not a big deal. I don't care about whatever thing has set her off."

"But you can't just give in to her all the time. She doesn't respect you and is trying to make you pay for her hurt feelings. You have feelings, too. There are always two sides to every argument, but it's not your job to protect her feelings from everything she doesn't like."

"I get that, but sometimes it's better to let something go now, because I'm playing a longer game. At some point, we have to get over our issues for the sake of our daughter."

It wasn't always easy to listen to this advice, but I realized I was too close to the situation. I wanted to avoid fights and animosity at all costs, but she was right that I needed to release myself from the guilt of divorce. It wasn't easy advice to take, but I always listened.

The minefield that I had to navigate was maintaining a working relationship with my daughter's mother while giving respect and deference to my new relationship. Jennifer and Stacey hated each other for reasons I didn't care to understand, and it was difficult keeping the peace at times. I don't think Jennifer appreciated the stress I was under, but her priority was to protect herself and her man, especially when her man was the focus of the issue.

Slowly but steadily, I came to appreciate the depths of Jennifer's loyalty to me. She'd never wanted to be a parent, but she took extra steps to make sure Yasmine was comfortable in our home. It wasn't the most natural fit for her, but she accepted the job as role model and parental figure. When I was buried with my two jobs and MBA studies, it was Jennifer that ran our home and made sure Yasmine was taken care of.

Being with her was the most complicated relationship I'd ever been in, but it was also the easiest. Our rules were clear and fair. I trusted her without reservation and knew the feeling was mutual. I loved her family as my own and was loved by them as if I were their own. As I retired my debts and approached my graduation date, I felt something I didn't think I'd ever feel again—the desire to get married.

After my marriage to Stacey, no one could blame me if I never ventured down that path again. I never thought I'd feel safe enough with someone to consider it an option, yet there I was. I knew marriage wasn't high on Jennifer's list, but we'd discussed the pros and cons of getting married. We'd already been together for almost two years and lived together for a year — we were basically married, minus the legalities. We'd also discussed moving from Tulsa to New York in the near future, so we considered the benefits that marriage would bring and found the idea natural and exhilarating.

Every time I considered taking the next step and purchasing a ring, however, a swirl of emotion filled me. I knew Jennifer was the right girl, but I was hesitant to trust my thoughts. I didn't want to compare her to any other woman, but it was impossible not to. She was wonderful to me, but what if I was making another mistake? What if I were following the same destructive tendencies that had plagued all my relationships? What if I wasn't strong enough to hold everything together?

I analyzed it until I was nearly crazy. Jennifer was my best friend, my lover, and my family. To marry her would be the greatest honor of my life, but I couldn't find the courage to buy the ring and finally ask her.

Eventually, I came to realize that my fear wasn't about

Jennifer or my love for her; it was about being sure I loved her for the right reasons. I was no longer the man who wanted to be with a woman for validation, or in an attempt to run away from my own pain.

With the decision made, I booked a roundtrip ticket to Dallas for the following day. I'd researched diamonds and ring styles for months before settling on a simple solitaire from Cartier, but the nearest store was in Dallas. I woke up an hour earlier than normal the next morning and dressed for work, claiming I had an early meeting. My return flight would arrive back in town around 4:30pm, thus making it seem as though I'd spent a normal day at work.

I felt bad lying to her, but it couldn't be helped. I'd never lied to her about anything. I knew it was for a good cause, but the notion of it still didn't feel right. I knew I was making the best decision I could, and was excited for what life was providing me.

After so much heartache, destruction, and lessons learned, I was happier than I ever imagined I could be. *I really hope this plane doesn't crash*, I thought, as the plane sped down the runway and lifted into the air.

Where Ever You Go, There You Are

The winter of 2012 was our first winter in New York as a married couple. Stacey and Yasmine had moved to Atlanta earlier in the year, and Yasmine was coming up for holiday visitation. She'd spent much of the summer with Jennifer and me, but she was excited to experience New York at Christmas.

I intended to take her ice skating for the first time. Jennifer had work to do, so it was only Yasmine and I. We considered Central Park and Bryant Park, but she wanted to go to Rockefeller Center. Even though it was more expensive, it was worth it to make my daughter happy.

We stood in front of the giant tree and sipped hot chocolate before taking our turn on the ice. We made several laps around the rink while we laughed and joked with each other. Despite the fun, I was cold and my feet hurt. I took refuge under the iconic golden statue while Yasmine continued to make laps.

I smiled as I watched my daughter skating around the same rink I'd seen all those years before as a poor child on the other side of the country. To that child, this place might as well have been on another planet, yet here I was. *The journey wasn't so bad*, I thought. Sure, there were ups and downs, but no one had promised life would be smooth and effortless.

I reflected on all of the happy times as well as the bad ones. There had been love and loss, abuse and triumphs, but I was thankful for all of it. My life was mine, and it had carried me to places beyond my wildest dreams.

"Daddy, come skate with me!" Yasmine called.

"I'm coming, baby girl," I said, joining her on the ice. "Did I ever tell you how much I wanted to skate here when I was a little boy?"

Author Bio

An independent business analyst on the Upper East Side of
Manhattan, Rahmaan (Roc) Mwongozi has cultivated a
successful career with Fortune 500 corporations including
Pfizer, Enron, and AT&T. His innovative approach to
problem-solving, however, began as a young boy in East
Oakland, when he vowed to leave poverty behind. Now living
a fulfilled life, Roc shares his story through motivational
speaking, podcasts, and his debut book, Inner Demons –
teaching how to apply systems analysis to problems that arise
in life and business

Contact Information
www.rocsworld.com
press@rocsworld.com
Twitter: @TheRocsWorld

CPSIA information can be obtained
at www.ICGtesting.com
Printed in the USA
FFHW021140071118
49304752-53538FF